GREAT PREACHING ON

PATRIOTISM

GREAT PREACHING ON

PATRIOTISM

COMPILED BY
CURTIS HUTSON

SWORD of the LORD
PUBLISHERS
P. O. BOX 1099, MURFREESBORO, TN 37133

Printed and Bound in the United States of America

Dedication

*Dedicated to all the brave men
who purchased our freedom at
Bunker Hill, Gettysburg, New Orleans,
Normandy Beach, Pearl Harbor
and Iwo Jima; also to those
who died for their country
in Korea and faraway Viet Nam*

Preface

Thankful? For America? Thankful for a continual rising cost of living? For an upsurge of crime? For a steadily decreasing moral code? For growing callousness among her people? For dishonesty in high places? For disintegrating home life?

Yes, thankful for America. We see a man on the television screen giving tender loving care to a wounded hawk, or risking his life to rescue an eagle or one of our four-footed animals and watch him receive praise on a national network. Thank You, Lord, that there are still individuals who care and have tender hearts toward the wounded and needy.

We read that America still leads the way in the sending out of missionaries, giving to needy nations, taking in refugees from every country, whether friend or foe. Thank You, Lord, for a nation that cares and gives.

When we travel in our cars, we do not need visas or passports to go from one state to another. No one is suspicious of our luggage. We are not followed or searched as we enter a public building, as some of us have been time and again in other countries. There are few restrictions on where we go or what we see. We may express our views freely in writing or speaking. We may meet openly to worship God with others, without fear of the secret police. Thank You, Lord, for freedom.

While there are necessary laws and controls in our society for the suppression of evil, if we break one of these laws, we are entitled to an attorney and a fair trial. Thank You, Lord, for justice.

We close the door of our home in the evening, not fearing a rude knock by the KGB, or some other organization, with resulting disappearance of one of our family members. Our children are safe with us, and we may train them according to the dictates of our hearts. We go to our jobs, establishing our own business if we prefer. Thank You, Lord, for privacy and personal enterprise.

Of course America has needs, our greatest being an old-time, sin-convicting, soul-saving, home-righting revival. The kind that father and mother used to have! A revival that counted it good business to take time for family worship each morning right in the middle of the wheat harvest. A revival that prompted them to quit work a half hour earlier on Wednesday so the whole family could get ready for prayer meeting. That's what America needs—more than anything else. Lord, grant it will come to pass in our generation!

Yes—there's a lot wrong with our country—but there's a lot right with it, too. It is still the best country in all the world. So we need to uphold it, pray for it, and be loyal to it.

Thank You, Lord, for America!

After reading this volume containing great messages on patriotism by a group of mighty men of the past and present, we sincerely believe you will pledge anew your allegiance to Old Glory! That you will become a flag-waving American! And that you will pray she will once again experience a great nationwide revival that will turn America back to God.

Here is the cream of the crop from the last fifty-three years' writing in THE SWORD OF THE LORD, America's foremost evangelistic publication. You will find no finer material in print on patriotism.

The last section, "This Is America!" though not a message but a compilation of happenings in America during her few short years of existence, contains scores of items you will have occasion to refer to again and again, items of extreme value to young and old, items not found elsewhere.

This Volume Number VII may prove to be the most popular in our GREAT PREACHING series.

—Sword of the Lord Publishers

Table of Contents

CURTIS W. HUTSON
1934–1995

ABOUT THE MAN:

In 1961 a mail carrier and pastor of a very small church attended a Sword of the Lord Conference, got on fire, gave up his route and set out to build a great soul-winning work for God. Forrest Hills Baptist Church of Decatur, Georgia, grew from 40 people into a membership of 7,900. The last four years of his pastorate there, the Sunday school was recognized as the largest in Georgia.

After pastoring for 21 years, Dr. Hutson—the great soul winner that he was—became so burdened for the whole nation that he entered full-time evangelism, holding great citywide-areawide-cooperative revivals in some of America's greatest churches. As many as 625 precious souls trusted Christ in a single service. In one eight-day meeting, 1,502 salvation decisions were recorded.

As an evangelist, he was in great demand.

At the request of Dr. John R. Rice, Dr. Hutson became Associate Editor of THE SWORD OF THE LORD in 1978, serving in that capacity until the death of Dr. Rice before becoming Editor, President of Sword of the Lord Foundation, and Director of Sword of the Lord Conferences. He continued in these ministries until his death on March 5, 1995, literally changing the lives of thousands of preachers and laymen alike, as well as winning many more thousands to Christ.

Dr. Hutson was the author of many fine books and booklets.

I.

America

CURTIS HUTSON

I am an American, and I love America. I want to speak on the subject, "America." I will say three things about it: first, about the greatness of America; second, about the God of America, and third, about the guilt of America.

I call your attention to Psalm 33:12:

"Blessed is the nation whose God is the Lord; and the people whom he hath chosen for his own inheritance."

That Bible verse is just as true as John 3:16. "Blessed is the nation whose God is the Lord." I'm afraid our leaders in this country, generally speaking, have forgotten the truth of this verse. The way to greatness is not found in the avenues we are pursuing; it is found in the simple truth of this statement: "Blessed is the nation whose God is the Lord."

I. THE GREATNESS OF AMERICA

God has given us in America wonderful natural resources. Practically every commodity that man uses can be found here. In the fields of America, every crop is grown. From the trees of America, every fruit and wood is secured. From the mines of America, every mineral that man uses is dug. And upon the prairies of America is every meat that is good for food.

God has also given us bountiful natural beauties. Every type of scenery that can be found in the world is seen in America.

When they talk about the beautiful coast of the Mediterranean, we can tell them of the Atlantic coast and the Pacific and Gulf shores.

When they talk about the Danube and the beautiful rivers of Europe, we can tell them of the beautiful Ohio, the St. Lawrence, the mighty Mississippi and the Colorado.

When they talk about the mountains of Switzerland, we can point them to the Alleghenies, the Adirondacks, the Smokies, the Rockies and others.

When they talk about the interesting spots in the world, we can tell them about Niagara Falls, the Grand Canyon, Yellowstone National Park, the Redwood Forest, Silver Springs and Stone Mountain down in Georgia.

There was a slogan when I was a boy, "See America first." I think that is good advice. You can put all the scenery of all the world together, and in my opinion we can match it right here in the United States of America. Ours is a beautiful country.

Not long ago my wife and I were driving to Murfreesboro, Tennessee. As we passed Chattanooga and were driving up I-24 toward Mur-freesboro, I couldn't help but notice the countryside. I very seldom see it when I fly—the homes, the country. How beautiful it is! God has blessed us with natural resources, and He has blessed America boun-tifully with natural beauty.

But God has also given us a good form of government, though we may not always use it as we should to its best potential. We have a free democracy. In the years that the United States has been a na-tion, the government of every large nation on earth has changed. But America's government, despite the attacks upon it, is still the same, with the Declaration of Independence and the Constitution still guarding our liberties. Yes, God has given us a good form of government.

God has also given us in America the freedom of speech and press. I can come to this platform and say whatever I wish without worrying about anyone harassing me. I can speak the convictions of my heart and not be worried about the policemen coming to take and lock me up.

The editor of the paper can write what he wishes in his column, week after week. He can downgrade America if he wishes. He has that freedom. Our good form of government has given it to him. If a preacher in Soviet Russia went to the pulpit and said what he wanted to say, the secret police would take him away, place him in a concentration camp, and only God knows what would then happen to him there. Yes, God has blessed America, and America is great.

God has also given us in America religious freedom. Whatever your belief, no one can close your church. It is sad, but even the homosexuals can have their own church by a freedom given them in

America. They can call it a homosexual church. It's far from the Bible, but that's a freedom they have in America.

Years ago in Spain they tried what is called the "fencing-off" theory, and in order to put Protestants out of business, they locked the doors of churches and closed one church after another trying to force them to union with the so-called Mother Church. We have never come to that in America.

I am concerned, and often I stay awake and pray, wondering how much longer we will have freedom in America. But for now we have, thank God, the freedom of speech and press. I wonder how long it will be before it is taken away from us. Someone said, "A man who won't use his freedom to defend his freedom doesn't deserve his freedom."

In Russia, on May 1, 1937, Stalin issued this decree: "There must not remain in the territory of Soviet Russia a single house of prayer, and the very conception of God will be banished from the boundaries of Russia." Yet in America we still have our religious freedom.

But where did we get this freedom? A humble Baptist preacher named Roger Williams, persecuted for his belief, fled to what is now known as the state of Rhode Island. There he founded the city of Providence, and in the Constitution of that state this Baptist preacher wrote, "Every man should be free to worship God according to the dictates of his own heart."

When Thomas Jefferson and others were forming the Constitution of the United States, they borrowed this principle and inserted it as a part of our Constitution. It came from a humble Baptist preacher named Roger Williams.

Yes, God has given us religious freedom in America.

And God has given us separation of church and state. Some do not understand what is meant by that expression. It means that no particular church is accepted as the "state church." Citizens of the country are not forced to pay taxes to support what is known as the "state church." We have no state religion in America. That is what separation of church and state means.

The separation of state and church does not mean that Christians are not to have interest in politics. We all have a God-given right and responsibility to vote when it comes time to elect the officials in our country. Every believer should exercise his God-given right very prayerfully, seeing that the right men are put in office in this country. It bothers me today that we have neglected this opportunity and in many cases have allowed the wrong men to get into office.

God give us in government some born-again, blood-washed believers who have a backbone made of iron and a will of steel, who will govern by Bible principles and who will stand up for the right things in this country.

If *somebody* doesn't do something *soon*, the greatness of America may be something of the past. We could be another country swallowed up by communism, under the dictatorship of an anti-God, anti-Bible, anti-Holy Spirit, communist dictator. Yes, God has given us a great country.

God has given us a country where everybody has a chance. Henry Ford once said to a group of young men, "There is no such thing as no chance."

Where but in America could an introvert like me build the largest church in the state of Georgia and the seventeenth largest in the nation; then go on to establish a Christian school, serve as president of a university and later become editor of THE SWORD OF THE LORD? Where in the world could a fellow go and have such an opportunity?

Thank God for America! Any poor country boy who has a dream can be something in America.

I heard Dr. B. R. Lakin say, "I used to plow a mule on the farm. Looking up to Heaven with tears coursing down my cheeks, I said, 'Dear God, someday I'll be something! Someday I'll be something!' " And that great preacher has crisscrossed America and preached in every state in the Union—in his own words, "like a little boy plowing out corn rows."

Thomas Edison was a poor boy, but today the whole world uses the 1,150 inventions that came from his mind and hand.

Yes, in America everybody has a chance. Everybody! No matter who you are, no matter what your educational background, if a fellow means business, he has a chance in America!

In 1800 someone made a suggestion that they close the patent office because everything that was going to be invented had already been invented. That was in 1800—before the automobile, before the telephone and before thousands and thousands of other things that we feel we couldn't live without today.

America—what a land of opportunity! Say what you will about it, I love it. I still cry when "The Star-Spangled Banner" is sung. I still stand straight and tall, and something wells up in my heart, when I salute the flag. I still appreciate America.

America is the only large nation that has never lost a war. We have never permanently given up an inch of territory except of our own free will. No other nation can make that boast. And the star-spangled banner is the only flag that has never stooped its proud head in defeat.

God has blessed America.

> **America! America!**
> **God shed His grace on thee**
> **And crown thy good with brotherhood**
> **From sea to shining sea.**

What a country we've got! We ought to love it, stand up for it and do what we can to help preserve the freedom we have in America! Now let me say a word about:

II. THE GOD OF AMERICA

If America is great, it's because, generally speaking, God has been given His rightful place in America.

A South American president once said to Roger Babson, "South America was founded by men who were seeking gold, but North America was founded by men who were seeking God."

Someone else said, "The Spaniards came here for gold; the French came here for gain; but the original colonists came here for God."

Pericles built a civilization upon culture, and it failed. Caesar built a civilization upon power, and it failed. Our forefathers founded our nation upon the Christian religion, and America will live so long as the Lord is still her God. Psalm 33:12 is still in the Bible: "Blessed is the nation whose God is the Lord." When we give God His rightful place again, we will see America blessed. "America. . .one nation, *under God!*" Oh, let's keep it like that.

When was the last time you prayed for those in government? When was the last time you prayed for America?

I want to go across this land and scream, "Wake up! Do something! Wake up!!" Let's give God His rightful place in America.

When the Pilgrims landed at Plymouth Rock, they knelt down upon the shore and thanked God for giving them this new country. The church of Jesus Christ was at the center of every new settlement in this land. When the Continental Congress faced great problems and difficulties and knew not which way to turn, Benjamin Franklin called upon the members of Congress to fall upon their knees and pray.

Not serried ranks with flags unfurled,
Nor armored ships that gird the world,
Not hoarded wealth, nor busy mills,
Not cattle on a thousand hills,
Not sages wise, nor schools nor laws,
Not boasted deeds in freedom's cause—
All these may be and yet the State
In the eye of God be far from great.
That land is great which knows the Lord,
Whose songs are guided by His Word.
Where justice rules 'twixt man and man,
Where love controls in art and plan,
Where breathing in his native air
Each soul finds joy in praise and prayer.
Thus may our country, good and great,
Be God's delight—man's best estate.

—Alexander Blackburn

Now a word about:

III. THE GUILT OF AMERICA

The first sin of America is indifference—just plain wicked indifference. We have said, "Well, I'm only one. I can't do anything." And we have allowed the Devil to take us further and further and further down the road of ruin.

Dr. Al Janney, speaking to fundamentalists, said, "We *will* get together. It's not a matter of whether or not we will get together; we will either get together on the outside of the fence or on the inside of the fence." Meaning by that, if we don't rise up now together and do something to preserve our great nation, soon the enemy will take over and put all of us behind the fence. And we will all get together. We'll be prisoners of the state. For God's sake, for the country's sake, for our kids' sake, let's get together outside the fence. It is time for us to shake off our indifference, rise up and do something!

When a good Christian runs for office, make sure you get out and vote for him, and do everything you can to get others to vote for him. And then, in America, I think we are guilty of ingratitude. Instead of thanking God for what we have, we want more. It's "Give me more, Lord! Give me more! More income, bigger pension, more welfare—and more handouts."

Ingratitude. Never stopping to thank God, just taking, taking, taking, taking.

Dr. Bob Jones, Sr., said, "The loveliest flower that blooms in the garden of the soul is gratitude; and when gratitude dies on the altar of a man's heart, he's well nigh gone." Show me a man who doesn't have proper gratitude, and I'll show you a man who is well nigh gone.

You know, I may be silly, but I still thank God for little things. I thank God for rugs on the floor. Man, we didn't have floors to put rugs on when I was coming up! Now I walk on carpet. Every once in awhile I stay in a motel room where they have carpet on the walls. And I say, "Look at this, man! We didn't even have a rug to put out front to wipe our feet on." We had to use an old burlap bag that the cow feed came in.

The guilt of indifference, the guilt of ingratitude and the guilt of iniquity! Just plain sin.

One Sunday night in 1939 in Paris, France, the Germans were storming the gates of the city. The people were in great danger. A newspaper man reported that more people went to church that day in Paris than at any other time since 1918. Isn't that a sad commentary? When the Germans were storming the gates of the city of Paris, that Sunday night more people went to church than had gone to church in 21 years! They were in great peril, and they went to church. Let bombs start falling on America, and we will suddenly become more religious. The churches will be filled to overflowing.

America needs God. America needs God in its government. America needs God in its businesses. And America needs God in her homes.

So long as there are homes to which men turn at close of day;
So long as there are homes where children are, where women stay;
If love and loyalty and faith be found across these sills,
A stricken nation can recover from its gravest ills.
So long as there are homes where fires burn and there is bread;
So long as there are homes where lamps are lit and prayers are said;
Although a people falter through the dark and nations grope,
With God Himself back of these little homes, we still have hope.

Yes, keep on praying. Keep on reading the Bible at the family altar. Keep on teaching Bible verses to the children. Keep on telling them it's wrong to smoke and dance and cuss and lie and drink and commit immorality. Keep on teaching the truth of the Bible. There is still hope.

America needs God in her schools. How badly we need Him! The sin in public schools has led many churches to start their own Christian school.

America needs God in her churches. Some churches are dead and dry and empty, and nothing ever happens. Nobody takes a stand, nobody preaches against sin—a little social sermonette for a bunch of Christianettes who run out and smoke their cigarettes, and nothing ever happens. We need God.

Several years ago Dr. Ayers, a medical missionary to China, said that on a certain Saturday afternoon the Chinese hospital was bombed by the Japanese. A number of the people were killed in the air raid, and part of the hospital was destroyed. On Sunday morning the people came together for an open-air service which was held in the hospital yard. The congregation stood about in the holes which were made by the bombs the day before. Here stood a boy who had lost an arm and whose parents had been killed on Saturday. Here was another who had lost his wife, and others who had suffered terribly; yet they met to worship God.

America needs God, not only in her homes and in government and in business, but she needs God in her churches. "Blessed is the nation whose God is the Lord."

America is guilty of many sins, but the guilt of America is our personal guilt. If America gets right with God, it will be when we as individuals get right with God.

Years ago I saw a cartoon in a newspaper where Uncle Sam was pictured on his knees praying. But if Uncle Sam ever gets on his knees to pray, it will be when the individual citizens of America are on their knees.

If we want to help this great country, then every one of us should get thoroughly right with God. Every sin should be confessed, and each of us should set out to live the best possible Christian life. The Bible says in Proverbs 14:34, "Righteousness exalteth a nation; but sin is a reproach to any people." But the nation can only be righteous when its citizens are righteous.

The Bible says in Psalm 33:12, "Blessed is the nation whose God is the Lord." But God is Lord of the nation as He is Lord of the individual life.

The greatest thing anyone can do to help this country is to be a good Christian. If you have not already trusted Jesus Christ as your Saviour, why not trust Him now? And then set out to live the Christian life.

V. RAYMOND EDMAN
1900-1967

ABOUT THE MAN:

V. Raymond Edman was born on May 9, 1900, in Chicago, where he received his early education. While attending Columbia University, service in the U.S Army interrupted. He later earned his B.A. degree from Boston University.

A missionary effort to the Quichua Indians in Ecuador drew Edman's energies from 1923-1928. His forced retirement due to climatic illness brought him back to the states.

While serving as a pastor and conducting a radio ministry in New England, he earned the M.A. and Ph.D. degrees in history from Clark University.

Sworn in as president of Wheaton College, Wheaton, Illinois, on May 9, 1940, Edman guided the college through 25 years of growth and advancement until 1965 when he became Chancellor, the office he held until his death.

Under Edman's tenure was the acquisition of a western campus in South Dakota, a modern science field station in the heart of the Black Hills; a northern campus for leadership training at Honey Rock Camp, a 400-acre woodland tract in Wisconsin; the Graduate School of Theology; and a cooperative nursing program with West Suburban Hospital, Oak Park, Illinois. Fourteen major buildings were erected on Wheaton Campus during his administration.

Always eager to represent the college, Edman traveled extensively in the states and abroad, and spoke on six of the seven continents. He was also a prolific writer, having authored 18 books.

He served on the Cooperating Board of the Sword of the Lord Foundation and was a Sword Book Club judge for many years.

His philosophy of living all of life "not somehow, but triumphantly" showed up in everything he did.

Some "Edmanisms" were: "It's always too soon to quit"; "Keep chin up and knees down"; "Never doubt in the dark what God told you in the light."

Dr. Edman died September 22, 1967, while speaking in chapel at college.

II.

The Ramparts We Watch

V. R. EDMAN

Statement of administrative policy given by President Edman to the Faculty of Wheaton College, Wheaton, Illinois, at its annual Autumn Workshop, Bethany Camp, Winona Lake, Indiana, September 8, 1947.

Our national anthem was born in darkness and danger; but when the night had passed, the "flag was still there."

No alarm nor exaggeration is needed to declare that our nation and the world are again in darkness, in dilemma more deep and in danger more desperate than in generations past.

In America the danger comes largely from within our own frontiers, much more so than from without. Nazi and Fascist have been overcome in mortal conflict; the communist abroad makes grimaces at the good way in American life but makes no material impact upon us from that distance.

Our foes are mingling among ourselves, and our "ramparts we must watch." If the body politic is healthy and strong, it need fear no foreign virus; if it is debilitated, it can be undermined and destroyed.

In national defense, each citizen must make his contribution to the general welfare. We at Wheaton have the responsibility of training a small segment of the next generation, while our Lord tarries; and we consider that task as containing possibilities for national good far in excess of the numbers we teach. Our efforts are multiplied by the lives touched by our students.

Life has never been easy nor ordinary in any generation, but in this day we face the apparent collapse of civilization because of unchecked forces running rampant in our reeling world. The challenge for the preparation of Christian young people to assume the responsibilities and opportunities of leadership in the Cause Worthwhile was never more imperative than at this hour.

We Defend Democracy

Our country came into being on a slowly rising tide of political liberalism. For several centuries Englishmen in the Mother Country and in the Colonies had contended against entrenched autocracy of English kings, especially the Stuarts with their pretensions to rule by divine right. Magna Carta (1215), Montfort's Parliament (1265), Model Parliament (1295), Petition of Right (1628), were milestones that pointed to the "Glorious Revolution" of 1688 and the Bill of Rights of the following year. By the latter, civil and political rights were acquired by the English people, and autocracy had been replaced by parliamentary government.

The liberal tradition took deep root in American life, where it flourished vigorously. Basic in colonial political thought were such concepts as the following: the natural rights of man, popular sovereignty, government by consent of the governed, civil liberties, supremacy of law ("a government of laws and not of men") and separation of political powers, so that no one branch of government should dominate the others. Colonial political thought was anti-autocratic at every point.

Political liberalism is basically and unequivocally opposed to autocracy. As such it is not intrinsically progressive or conservative. When despotism dominates the existing regime, the liberal is an ardent reformer; when free government drifts toward autocracy, he is a conservative, resisting all efforts to destroy democracy.

True liberalism consists of two fundamental concepts: democracy ("that form of government in which the ruling power of a State is legally vested, not in any particular class or classes, but in the members of the community as a whole"[1]), and individualism ("which implies the right of each person to control his own actions as long as he does not seriously interfere with the liberty or the actions of others"[2]). Both are basic in American political philosophy.

Infused into our national Constitution are the great political principles, developed and defined in the course of that long struggle of liberalism against autocracy. These principles include:

(1) **Popular sovereignty,** meaning that political power resides in the people and that government is by the consent of the governed;

(2) **Constitutional government,** in which all law must conform to fundamental law and all action must be according to law;

(3) **Federalism,** in which delegated and defined powers are granted to the national government and residual powers retained by the States;

(4) **Limited government,** one having a constitutional limitation as

to the division of powers between the national government and the States, and as to the personal and property rights of the individual citizen (e.g., in the Bill of Rights);

(5) **Delegated powers,** in which is defined the scope of action that can be exercised by the federal government; and

(6) **Separation of powers,** in which each branch of the government is independent in its sphere of action and yet by "checks and balances" there is maintained effective interaction among them, lest concentration of power in any branch threaten the interest of all the people.

Not lightly nor idly were these principles fashioned; rather they were forged on the anvil of long and bitter struggle. The liberties which our fathers won for us are now in danger of being lost because all the world is turning back toward autocracy, and we are either indifferent or uninformed on the essential and intrinsic excellencies of the democratic way of life. Eternal vigilance is ever the price of freedom.

The rampart of political liberty we must watch. In this connection, the American Political Science Association makes the following pertinent comment:

> Where was it that the founders of the union and the authors of the Constitution learned the principles of sound government? Granting that they had great native talent and inventiveness; nevertheless, Hamilton, Madison, Jefferson and other men of their stature learned what they knew from the books of scholars and from the teachers under whom they sat in college and also from experience and reflection. The leaders of each generation, the public servants and the rank and file of the citizens apply in public affairs what they learn in their schools, colleges and universities. Woe unto that democratic nation whose teachers and students of politics do not hold fast to the truth of today, and yet keep ahead of the majority in visualizing the needs of tomorrow.[3]

We Defend the American Way of Life

We should not be intimidated by cynicism nor bewildered by propaganda. For a generation, alleged intellectuals have "debunked" the Founding Fathers of our Republic, with the insinuation that nothing of permanent value was contributed by those who struggled and suffered to bring a new government into being and have cast aspersions on the freedom of the individual which underlies our way of life.

We must not be confused by slogans; rather, we must face the realities.

Democracy, in the succinct statement of Abraham Lincoln, is a "government of the people, by the people, and for the people." It alone provides for the maximum of individual liberty and responsibility. **Socialism,** by its very definition ("a political and economic theory of social reorganization, the essential feature of which is governmental control of economic activities . . . ."[4]) is an enhancement of governmental powers, **at the expense of every individual.** Our fathers learned that government is by nature arbitrary, and that an accumulation of power is in the long run injurious to the citizen.

Have men taken to heart the sad lesson of Germany? For when Hitler came to power, one of his first moves was to destroy trade unionism. National socialism became national arsenic!

Democracy offers a maximum of individual liberty and a minimum of governmental regulations; socialism gives individual liberty and more government; communism gives all government and no individual liberty worth mentioning.

Communism is the opposite of the system of private property and rights, and it reduces the individual to mere insignificance. The state is everything; the individual is nothing. By the illusion of economic equality, men become the slaves of the state; their condition is more pitiable than that of the serfs of former days.

The democratic way of life seeks to raise the standard of living and the rights of all; communism seeks to level all downward to a common party.

The upward look contrasts sharply with the downward! Regulation does not liberate; it reforges the chains that were broken in the long struggle for democracy and liberty.

The principles of Marxian Socialism (the fundamental doctrine of communism) have been insinuated into American thinking, and their implications have not been faced by many. The materialistic concept of history, the doctrine of class struggle, the dictatorship of the proletariat, the nationalization of all property and reward according to need, worldwide revolution and the dismissal of religion as merely a baneful "opiate": these are basic postulates of communism and are diametrically opposed to free enterprise and government of free men.

Is it true that property collectively owned and administered by public officials without personal profit to themselves causes social antagonism to disappear? Is social progress promoted by strife or by cooperation? Do exploitation, acquisitiveness and social antagonisms disappear simply by transfer of title from the individual to the state? Does communism revolutionize human nature so that all diversities of interest and ability are adjusted amicably? Cannot collective property be administered for the benefit of a class? Does not the apparent harmony in a communist state arise from the authority of the dictator rather than from the natural harmonization of diverse interests?

Is it not true that the abolition of private property by communism establishes a new kind of property—namely, the public office that controls collective capital; so that the struggle for wealth becomes in effect a struggle for power?

Is it not true that dictatorship, terror and conscription of life and labor are indigenous to the communist state and not merely a passing phase?

The fundamentals should be faced squarely. Communism is essentially regulation and regimentation of the many by the few; in other words, old autocracy with a new face. It promises freedom by making a serf of the individual, whose chains bear the euphemistic title of a new freedom.

Names do not remove chains. At every point, communism is at odds with the tradition of liberal economic and political thought that made America free and great. Our fathers learned by long and bitter experience that concentration of political authority is always injurious to the best interest of all. Autocracy always becomes tyranny.

Communism is autocracy, we repeat, and the antithesis of democracy.

The problem reduces itself to this further basic concept: all collectivist theory in one way or another denies the inviolability of the individual. For that reason collectivism communistic or fascistic—is always anti-religious, and logically so. In the thoughtful words of a careful student:

> Collectivist regimes are always profoundly irreligious. For religious experience entails the recognition of an inviolable essence in men; it cultivates a self-respect and a self-reliance which tend at some point to resist the total subjection of the individual to any earthly power. By the religious experience, the humblest communicant is led into the presence of a power so much greater than his master's that the distinctions of this world are of little importance.
>
> So it is no accident that the only open challenge to the totalitarian state has come from men of deep religious faith. For in their faith they are vindicated as immortal souls, and from this enhancement of their dignity they find the reason why they must offer a perpetual challenge to the dominion of men over men.

It must always be the ambition of the despot to destroy religion if
he cannot exploit it as an instrument of his power. . . . In the powerful national collectivist states of our time, the sins of the clergy have
been a pretext, seized upon by the collectivists in their determination
to stamp out the ultimate resistance of the human soul. The real reason
for the irreligion of fascists and communists is that religion cultivates
a respect of men as men. Against that respect the totalitarian state
cannot long prevail.[5]

The ramparts of economic and social liberty we must watch. The
general tide is away from freedom and toward bondage. Let us face
frankly and fearlessly the alternatives graphically and accurately
presented by Mr. Lippmann:

Everywhere the movements which bid for men's allegiance are
hostile to the movements in which men struggled to be free. The programs of reform are everywhere at odds with the liberal tradition. Men
are asked to choose between security and liberty. To improve their
fortunes they are told that they must renounce their rights. To escape
from want they must enter a prison. To regularize their work they must
be regimented. To obtain greater equality they must have less freedom.
To have national solidarity they must oppress the dissenters. To
enhance their dignity they must lick the boots of tyrants. To realize
the promise of science they must destroy free inquiry. To promote
the truth they must not let it be examined.

These choices are intolerable. Yet these are the choices offered by
the influential doctrinaires of the contemporary world. Thus those who
would be loyal to the achievements of the past are in general disposed
to be fatalistically complacent about the present, and those who have
plans for the future are prepared to disown the heroic past. It is a
vicious dilemma.[6]

It is a dilemma we cannot minimize nor avoid. We must face its issues
and implications. Autocracy in any form—fascist or communist—
collectivism of any kind, deny the intrinsic worth and status of the individual and destroy the liberties that have been achieved in the long
course of man's struggle for human rights. Autocracy and collectivism
are alley-ways to bondage, not highways of freedom.

We Defend Christianity

One's first reaction to the statement, "We defend Christianity," is,
"Christianity needs no defense." It was Spurgeon who declared that
Christianity, like a lion, can defend itself. However, Christianity is

subject to heavy and bitter attacks by its many foes; and we need to know what we defend and why and how.

Again, the definition of terms is essential to the discussion. Christianity is defined as "the religion of Christians; the system of doctrines and precepts taught by Christ; hence, the body of beliefs, practices and sentiments developed from the teachings and life of Christ."[4]

At Wheaton we hold that Christianity is the revelation of God in the Scriptures and in the Lord Jesus Christ, whereby the Redeemer is presented to mankind. In view of the efforts to undermine or explain away the historic Christian faith by discrediting the Scriptures or giving unwarranted interpretations thereto, we have found it necessary to state our faith in positive, unequivocal language. The nine-point statement contained in our catalog is the official testimony of the college, and to it the trustees, administration and faculty subscribe without any mental qualification:

1. We believe in the Scriptures of the Old and New Testaments as verbally inspired by God and inerrant in the original writing, and that they are of supreme and final authority in faith and life.

2. We believe in one God, eternally existing in three Persons: Father, Son and Holy Spirit.

3. We believe that Jesus Christ was begotten by the Holy Spirit, born of the Virgin Mary, and is true God and true man.

4. We believe that man was created in the image of God; that he sinned and thereby incurred, not only physical death, but also that spiritual death which is separation from God; and that all human beings are born with a sinful nature and, in the case of those who reach moral responsibility, become sinners in thought, word and deed.

5. We believe that the Lord Jesus Christ died for our sins, according to the Scriptures, as a representative and substitutionary sacrifice; and that all who believe in Him are justified on the ground of His shed blood.

6. We believe in the resurrection of the crucified body of our Lord, in His ascension into Heaven and in His present life there for us, as High Priest and Advocate.

7. We believe in "that blessed hope," the personal, premillennial and imminent return of our Lord and Saviour Jesus Christ.

8. We believe that all who receive by faith the Lord Jesus Christ are born again of the Holy Spirit and thereby become children of God.

9. We believe in the bodily resurrection of the just and the unjust, the everlasting blessedness of the saved and the everlasting punishment of the lost.[7]

Christianity has been subjected to attack throughout its long career in human history. In the early centuries of its spread, it was attacked largely as to the Person of the Lord Jesus Christ, especially as to His essential deity. The brunt of attack in the past generations has shifted largely from the Redeemer to the Revelation of God in the Scriptures themselves on the ground that, if we have no adequate or accurate revelation, then the Person of Christ and all of historic Christianity goes by default.

The attack on the Scriptures has come from several sources. The loud denunciations of leaders in the *Age of Reason*, Voltaire, Paine, and the like, produced noise but little real impact against the foundations of the Christian faith. Paine could rant that Christianity was "too absurd for belief, too impossible to convince and too inconsistent to practice," but thoughtful people came to realize that the atheist was violently prejudiced and absurdly uninformed.[8] There are those who repeat parrot-like and viciously the specious arguments of that day.[9]

More scholarly and subtle was the attack of the higher criticism against the text of the Scriptures. Although the "higher critics" seek to undermine the validity and authority of the Bible, not all by any means are so bold as some who declare,

> What I mean when I say that the Old Testament was "forged" will be fairly clear . . . . the critical theory is that not a single book of the Old Testament, as we have it, is older than the Ninth Century (B.C.) and that in the Fifth Century all the older books and fragments were combined together into the Old Testament as we have it and were drastically altered so as to yield a version of early Hebrew history which is not true.[10]
>
> The simple fact is that the New Testament, as we know it, is a helter-skelter accumulation of more or less discordant documents, some of them probably of respectable origin but others palpably apocryphal, and that most of them, the good along with the bad, show unmistakable signs of having been tampered with.[11]

Astonishing assurance of the critics who brush away the Rock of Revelation with a wave of the hand!

In reply to those attacks, let us hear the findings of patient and trustworthy scholars.

The late Dr. Robert Dick Wilson of Princeton, who prepared for his life work by fifteen years of language study (in which he became a master of Babylonian, Ethiopian, Phoenician, all the Aramaic dialects, Egyptian, Coptic, Persian, Armenian, Arabic, Syriac and others, twenty-six in all) and then by fifteen years of biblical textual study in the light of his findings in philology, came to

> . . .the conviction that **no man knows enough to assail the truthfulness of the Old Testament.** Wherever there is sufficient documentary evidence to make an investigation, the statements of the Bible, in the original text, have stood the test.[12]

In regard to the New Testament: it has been said by a careful and competent scholar:

> The question, "Shall we hear evidence or not?" presents itself at the threshold of every investigation of the New Testament. Modern criticism for a time entered on its task with a decided negative. Its mind was made up, and it would not listen to evidence on a matter that was already decided.
>
> But the results of recent exploration made this attitude untenable. . . . The Nineteenth Century critical method was false and is already antiquated. . . . The history of literary criticism of ancient documents during the last fifty years has demonstrated that by such purely verbal criticism one can prove anything and nothing. Almost all the real progress that has been made has come from the discovery of new evidence and not from verbal criticism of the old books.[13]

There lurks in many a mind the latent thought that somehow science has disproved and displaced Christianity. Science deals with the material, the evident, the positive, the definite, in terms of mathematical exactness. Some have declared that because they cannot find God in a test tube, He does not exist, not realizing the limitation of observation and experience that marks every life. Who has been everywhere, forever, to know there is no God? For that matter, who ever found love or loyalty or patriotism in a test tube, not to speak of countless other values?

It seems that mankind by and large prefers unbelief to faith in God. The Scriptures declare that attitude in many places. The Lord Jesus declared:

"This is the condemnation, that light is come into the world, and men loved darkness rather than light, because their deeds were evil."—John 3:19.

"Because that, when they knew God, they glorified him not as God, neither were thankful. . . . professing themselves to be wise, they became fools."—Rom. 1:21,22.

Men have a bias against God because they desire not to have His truth in their consciousness. There is the will to unbelief. Witness the testimony of H. G. Wells:

> I was indeed a prodigy of Early Impiety. I was scared by Hell, I did
> not at first question the existence of Our Father, but no fear nor terror
> could prevent my feeling that His All-Seeing Eye was that of an Old
> Sneak. . . . there was a time when I believed there was a Devil, but
> there was never a time when I did not heartily detest the whole
> business.[14]

As to anything miraculous in the ministry of Christ, the outstanding
church historian of the Nineteenth Century declared flatly, "We do not
believe, and we shall never believe."[15]

This generation is well described as "an age of unbelief," as stated
by President Angell of Yale in his baccalaureate sermon to the class
of 1930:

> The period in which we are living may well come to be known in
> religious history as "the age of unbelief"; the latest of any, for the
> lineage runs direct and substantially uninterrupted from the Greek
> philosophers to the Fourth Century (B.C.) with occasional later high
> points such as the British skepticism of the Eighteenth Century and
> the radical movements of the French Revolution. . . . I doubt whether
> any vital element in Christianity, to say nothing of other religions, has
> wholly escaped this assault.[16]

Of this assault we are not unfamiliar, nor are we afraid. Men have
always fought the fact of the supernatural in creation, revelation and
redemption. A leading American anthropologist declared boldly,

> In truth from the period of the early ages of Greek thought, man
> has been eager to discover some natural cause of evolution and to
> abandon the idea of supernatural invention in the order of nature.[17]

Various theories have been propounded over the centuries; and one
by one they have proved untenable. Evolution is the latest in the long
course of human unbelief, and thinking men are less sure of it today
than a generation ago. Some cling to it because its only alternative is
creationism.

The revelation of God in the Scriptures has been attacked from every
angle: its text, history, language, chronology, human authorship; but
one by one the objections are met fully and with finality by the patient
and unbiased scholar, in the manuscripts and memorials of antiquity.
Languages of a forgotten yesterday are unlocked and cast light on
obscure words in the text of Holy Writ. The archaeologist finds evidence
to corroborate the Scripture but not to contradict it.

We defend Christianity because we have found it to be true for ourselves, and we want others to find its truth and power. We have found the Lord Jesus Christ to be an adequate and effective Saviour from the penalty and power of sin. We have found the Bible to be the Word of the Living God, in whose light we have found light in time and, we are sure, in eternity. Through the Scriptures and the Saviour we have come to know true peace: "peace with God" and "the peace of God which passeth all understanding." We do not understand everything, far from it; but although we "now see through a glass, darkly. . . . [and] know in part," we have found the Christian, theistic view of the world and of man to provide systematic, symmetrical, satisfying and sufficient center for ourselves and our universe.

Summary

Democracy, that "government of the people, by the people, and for the people,"[18] which form of government derives its "just powers from the consent of the governed";[19] **freedom,** political, social, economic, religious; and **Christianity** are indigenous and indispensable in the American way of life.

The Founding Fathers, beginning with Separatist and Puritan in Massachusetts, brought with them the seeds of all three. The desire for freedom that impelled them to leave familiar scenes for stern and rock-bound coasts, was basically theological in its immediate origins; but it gathered economics and politics to itself to break every shackle of superstition and feudalism.

They were heirs of the Reformation and unleavened by the Renaissance. They had the problem of reforging, in the heat of controversy and the struggle for existence, a new pattern of political and social organization that should adjust equitably the rights of the individual and the needs of the state.

> The final end and outcome of their concern for a more equitable relation of the individual to society was the principle of a democratic commonwealth, established in the conception of political equalitarianism. . . .
>
> There was gunpowder packed away in Luther's doctrine of the priesthood of all believers, and the explosion that resulted made tremendous breaches in the walls of a seemingly impregnable feudalism. . . .
>
> On the whole it is no mistake to regard the Puritan revolution as primarily a rebellion of the capable middle class whose growing trade

interest demanded a larger measure of freedom than a paternal king and a landed aristocracy were willing to grant; and its significant contributions to the modern world were the two systems it did so much to further: the system of capitalism and the system of parliamentary government.[20]

Of the Separatists, the radicals of the seventeenth century, it could be added,

Counsels of social expediency were accounted as dust in the balance against the explicit commandment of the Lord to separate from the sins of the world; and clinging to the text of the Scripture the Separatist was led straight to the conception of a Christian democracy.[21]

The interdependence of free government, free people and vital Christianity is nowhere expressed more definitely and accurately than in the public statements of our first President, George Washington. In his first Inaugural Address he declared at the outset:

It would be peculiarly improper to omit in this first official act my fervent supplications to the Almighty Being who rules over the universe, who presides in the councils of nations and whose providential aids can supply every human defect, that His benediction may consecrate to the liberties and happiness of the people of the United States a government instituted by themselves for those essential purposes and may enable every instrument employed in its administration to execute with success the functions allotted to his charge.[22]

In his earnest and eloquent Farewell Address fashioned out of long observation and experience, he wrote:

Of all the dispositions and habits which lead to political prosperity, religion and morality are indispensable supports . . . and let us with caution indulge the supposition that morality can be maintained without religion. Whatever may be conceded to the influence of refined education or minds of peculiar structure, reason and experience both forbid us to expect that national morality can prevail in exclusion of religious principle.[23]

These are the ramparts we watch: freedom of the individual from arbitrary and autocratic government; freedom of the individual from economic and social restriction, but always for the welfare of all as well as for that of himself; and the freedom of the Gospel, whose truth makes us free indeed!

Bibliography

[1]Bryce, James, *Modern Democracies* (MacMillan Co., 1921), Vol. 1, p. 20.

[2]McGovern, William Montgomery, *From Luther to Hitler: The History of Fascist-Nazi Political Philosophy* (Houghton Mifflin Co., 1941), p. 12.

[3]American Political Science Association, *Political Science and the World of Tomorrow* (1946), p. 1.

[4]Lippman, Walter, *An Inquiry Into the Principles of the Good Society* (Little, Brown & Co., 1938), pp. 382, 383.

[5]*Ibid.*, (Introduction, pp. x, xi).

[6]*Webster's New International Dictionary.*

[7]Bulletin of Wheaton College, *Catalog Number 1946-47*, p. 10.

[8]One remembers Theodore Roosevelt's exacting and objective comment that Paine was "a dirty atheist," dirty mentally and physically. Smith, Wilbur M., *Therefore Stand* (Boston: W. A. Wilde Co., 1945), p. 170.

[9]For example, Hinton, Richard W., *Arsenal for Skeptics* (New York: Alfred A. Knopf, 1934).

[10]McCabe, Joseph, *The Story of Religious Controversy* (Boston: The Strafford Co., 1929), p. 126.

[11]Mercken, H. L., *A Treatise on the Gods* (New York: Alfred A. Knopf, 1930), p. 209.

[12]Wilson, Robert Dick, *Is the Higher Criticism Scholarly?* (Philadelphia: The Sunday School Times Co., 1922), p. 10.

[13]Ramsay, W. M., *Luke the Physician,* and other Studies in the History of Religion (London: Hodder and Stoughton, 1908), pp. 3, 4, 8, 59.

[14]Wells, H. G., *Experiment in Autobiography* (New York: MacMillan Co., 1934), p. 45.

[15]Harnack, W., *What Is Christianity?* (New York: Putman Co., 1901, English Trad. 2nd Edition), p. 30.

[16]Angell, James Rowland, in *New York Times,* June 16, 1930.

[17]Osborn, Henry Fairfield, *The Origin and Evolution of Life* (New York: Charles Scribner's Sons, 1917), p. ix.

[18]Lincoln, Abraham, *Gettysburg Address.*

[19]Jefferson, Thomas, *Declaration of Independence in Congress,* July 4, 1776.

[20]Parrington, Vernon Lewis, *Main Currents in American Thought* (New York: Harcourt, Brace & Co., 1927), Vol. 1, p. 6.

[21]*Ibid.*, p. 9.

[22]Richardson, James D., *A Compilation of the Messages and Papers of the Presidents* (Washington: Bureau of National Art & Literature, 1910), Vol. 1, p. 44.

[23]*Ibid.*, p. 212.

1901-1984
BASCOM RAY LAKIN

ABOUT THE MAN:

On June 5, 1901, a baby boy was born to Mr. and Mrs. Richard Lakin in a farmhouse on Big Hurricane Creek in the hill country of Wayne County, West Virginia. Mrs. Lakin had prayed for a "preacher man" and had dedicated this baby to the Lord even before he was born.

Lakin was converted in a revival meeting at age 18. Following his conversion, he became a Baptist preacher. With a mule for transportation, he preached in small country churches in the mountains and hills of West Virginia and Kentucky. The transportation changed as well as the size of his congregations.

In 1939, he became associate pastor of Cadle Tabernacle, Indianapolis, and upon the death of Founder Cadle, became pastor of that once great edifice of evangelism that seated 10,000, and had a choir loft of 1,400. Lakin preached to over 5,000 on Sunday mornings and half that many on Sunday nights.

Cadle Tabernacle had no memberships. It was a radio-preaching center broadcasting from coast to coast. In those fourteen years there, Ray Lakin became a household word across America.

In 1952, he entered full-time evangelism. His ministry carried him around the world, resulting in an estimated 100,000 conversions, and legion the number entering the ministry.

He was the preacher's friend, the church's helper, the common man's leader, and for sixty-five years, God's mighty messenger.

He was one of the most sought-after gospel preachers in America. On March 15, 1984, the last of the old-time evangelists took off for Glory. He would soon have been 83.

III.

America's Greatest Need

B. R. LAKIN

The following sermon by Dr. B. R. Lakin entitled "America's Greatest Need" was read into the Congressional Record by the Honorable Congressman William Jennings Bryan Dorn of South Carolina on October 3, 1968. Congressman Dorn made the following introductory remarks before reading the sermon:

"Mr. Speaker, it was my great privilege to attend the Haven of Rest Mission's eighth anniversary dinner on Saturday night, September 21, 1968, at the Holiday Inn, Anderson, South Carolina.

"My warm personal friend, the Reverend Hugh Parsons, founder and superintendent of the Haven Rescue Mission and Children's Home, has the answer to poverty, disease and moral decay so evident in our country today. His mission is a classic example of what can be done and what is right and good about America. Mr. Parson's anniversary banquet was an occasion I will long remember. My friend, Rev. Robert Martin, was Master of Ceremonies. Many distinguished political leaders, ministers and members of the Mission Board were present to hear the following outstanding and timely address by Dr. B. R. Lakin of Fort Gay, West Virginia."

* * * *

"The Lord liveth, in truth, in judgment, and in righteousness; and the nations shall bless themselves in him, and in him shall they glory."— Jer. 4:2.

In these days of national strife and international confusion, when the seeds of hatred are being cultivated in the hotbeds of communism and radicalism, let us throw back our shoulders, double up our fists, rough with the callouses of honest toil, and stand up for true, fundamental, godly Americanism.

The Bible teaches patriotism, and patriotism was the light that burned in the hearts of the faithful in the midnight gloom of the dark ages. It was the torch that lit the fires of the Reformation. It was the rock upon which Western civilization was founded. And if our civilization survives the onslaught of the Red Scourge, it will be Christian patriotism that will fuel the lamps of truth and provide morale for the fight for freedom.

America has many privileges, but it also has great responsibilities. Our freedom was obtained at a great price. Our first responsibility is to God, but we are duty-bound to our beloved country.

"Let every soul be subject unto the higher powers. For there is no power but of God: the powers that be are ordained of God."—Rom. 13:1.

Sir Walter Scott struck a note of true Christian patriotism when he wrote—

> **Breathes there a man, with soul so dead,**
> **Who never to himself hath said,**
> **This is my own, my native land!**
> **Whose heart hath ne'er within him burn'd,**
> **As home his footsteps he hath turn'd**
> **From wandering on a foreign strand?**
> **If such there breathe, go mark him well;**
> **For him no minstrel raptures swell;**
> **High though his titles, proud his name,**
> **Boundless his wealth as wish can claim—**
> **Despite those titles, power and pelf,**
> **The wretch, concentred all in self,**
> **Living, shall forfeit fair renown,**
> **And, doubly dying, shall go down**
> **To the vile dust from whence he sprung,**
> **Unwept, unhonor'd, and unsung.**

With manmade creeds forgotten, we find common ground in the sublime truth of the "Old Book" and in the spirit of those brave men who crossed the seas in search of a free land in which they could worship their God according to the dictates of their hearts.

We enjoy the benefits of a land founded in faith, baptized in blood and dedicated to the freedom of worship. I would like, by the help of the Spirit, to revive within our hearts some of the great ideals that have made America the "Hub," the very center upon which the world revolves. I would like to stir up our souls with a renewed national zeal and a closer walk with God, without whom no nation can succeed.

I. WE NEED A SENSE OF GRATITUDE

One day in every year we celebrate Thanksgiving, but one day out of 365 is not enough. Americans should thank God every day that we live in "the land of the four freedoms." Every day we should thank God for the sacrifice of blood, sweat, privation, even death, on the part of the multiplied thousands of our heroic dead. Had it not been for their standing between us and the iron hand of fascism and Nazism, we might not be commemorating their sacrifice. Instead, we might be goose-stepping at the heels of storm troopers and taking our orders from them instead of the Bible being read in our beloved homes. *Mein Kampf* might now be our textbook. Instead of blending our free voices in the singing of "My Country, 'Tis of Thee," we might be "Heiling" and saluting the swastika.

Let us bow our heads in humility and our hearts in reverence and gratitude to a merciful God who has brought us national deliverance.

A. We should be grateful for the righteous birth of our native land.

Other nations were born in the blood of plundering conquest, but not America. Our nation was conceived in the noble hearts of courageous, righteous men. She was born in the throes of holy prayer at Plymouth Rock, cradled by the strong hand of stalwart faith, nourished at the bosom of living, vital, sincere religion, fed on the wholesome food of the highest ideals and developed to her towering stature under the smiling approval of Almighty God.

America stands today a fortress of freedom, loved by all free men, respected by the liberty-loving peoples of the earth, feared by the enemies of God and human liberty. With the shadows of communism deepening upon every continent, America holds high the torch of faith, light and hope for the downtrodden peoples of the world.

B. We should be grateful for our natural, industrial and scientific resources with which we have been blessed.

Because of our giving God His rightful place at the outset of our national life, God smiled—and gold poured from the rocky crags of the Golden West.

God smiled—and wide acres of grain sprang from the soil of the Middle West.

God smiled—and the picturesque hills of the East yielded black gold in ample abundance to warm our hearths and turn the wheels of industry.

God smiled—and the automobile, the airplane and a thousand and one industrial miracles took place before our very eyes.

God smiled—and has seen to it that Old Glory has never dipped her colors to any atheistic, God-hating, man-enslaving country.

God smiled—and our scientists brought into being the atomic and nuclear bombs, which are destined to be that paradoxical instrument of destruction to save men from destruction.

Today, we stand in a precarious position in regard to our national life.

We as a nation must do nothing to invoke the frown of Almighty God. Our course must be such as to keep Heaven's smile upon our beloved country.

We stand at the crossroads. To the left lie the bogs of extreme liberalism, socialism and the inevitable drift into communism. To the right lie the time-worn swamps of ultra-conservatism, which leads to monopolies of certain groups at the expense of other groups.

We must keep in the middle of the road and prayerfully seek the guidance of God or our nation will go the way of all other nations in past history—in oblivion.

It is the approval of God that makes a country great, not the genius of statesmen, not merely the form of government nor the energy of its people, but the level of the national morals and the depth of national faith in God.

> Not serried ranks with flags unfurled,
> Not armored ships that gird the world,
> Not hoarded wealth nor busy mills,
> Not cattle on a thousand hills,
> Nor sages wise, nor schools nor laws,
> Not boasted deeds in Freedom's cause—
> All these may be, and yet the state
> In the eye of God be far from great,
> That land is great which knows the Lord,
> Whose songs are guided by His Word;
> Where justice rules, 'twixt man and man,
> Where love controls in art and plan;
> Where, breathing in His native air,
> Each soul finds joy in praise and prayer—
> Thus may our country, good and great,
> Be God's delight—man's best estate.

C. We should be thankful for our homes.

Though many of our citizens have brought reproach on the American home by their selfish and loose living, it still remains our greatest heritage. The meaning of the word *home* is so foreign to some peoples of the world that the equivalent of the word is not even in their language. The American traveler abroad, when he sees the condition existing in some foreign families, comes into a new appreciation of our home life in this country.

Henry Van Dyke once wrote after a trip abroad,

So it's home again, and home again, America for me!
My heart is turning home again, and there I long to be,
In the land of youth and freedom beyond the ocean bars,
Where the air is full of sunlight and the flag is full of stars.

Thank God for a part in guiding the American home in spiritual things! For years, every morning a radio poll showed I spoke to 800,000 people over the Nation's Family Prayer Period. People from all walks of life gathered before their radios at the beginning of the new day to look into His face and listen to His Word. We need a revival of interest in spiritual matters today.

II. WE NEED A GREATER CONSCIOUSNESS OF OUR RESPONSIBILITY

Our greatest sin as a nation is the sin of complacency. Smugness is the forerunner of indifference, and indifference is the predecessor of national deterioration. As the old saying goes, "A chain is no stronger than its weakest link." It can be truthfully stated that America is no stronger than her weakest citizen. This truth puts a tremendous responsibility upon every one of us.

The forces of anti-Americanism and anti-Christianity are at work in our beloved land. Most of their work is sinister and under cover; but, like leaven, they seek to eventually leaven the whole lump of our way of life and supplant regimented, centralized totalitarianism for old-fashioned, red-blooded, stalwart Americanism.

This leaven of atheism is found in high places as well as low. No nation ever survived a moral collapse. When Rome was in the zenith of her power and glory, sin started to eat like a canker at the heart of her national morals. Her politicians became weak, flabby and spineless. She became morally weak and spiritually depraved.

One night while the Roman politicians were engaged in a shameful, drunken orgy in the resort town of Pompeii, the fires of God's judgment were raging not far distant in the bowels of famous old Mt. Vesuvius, the volcanic mountain. As the night wore on, the sin and debauchery became more pronounced in Pompeii. There came a weird, sickly rumbling from the adjacent mountain. For years Vesuvius had been quiet and asleep, but the hour of God's judgment had arrived. As the revelers continued their sinful indulgence, Vesuvius quivered with a mighty quake, and the top of the volcano was blown completely away as a surging river of flaming, molten rock poured down the mountain in a death-dealing torrent.

There was no hope of escape. The door of God's mercy was closed for these Roman renegades. As the lava swiftly overwhelmed the city, 25,000 people were buried beneath the flood of molten rock.

This was the beginning of Rome's end as a nation. It all began when sin and lust supplanted the love for God and when gratification of the lower appetites took the place of noble character.

Egypt was once the center of world culture, and their scientists were way ahead in scientific knowledge and research. But Egyptian civilization floundered upon the rocks of immorality and depravity, and today she is leagues behind other nations which have striven to give God His rightful place in their national development. One has only to walk the streets of Cairo and note the lust and the sin on every hand, to see the reason for her utter lack of national prosperity and integrity. A nation can rise no higher than the moral level of her average individual.

Every American, in these days of confusion and moral crisis, has an individual responsibility to God and his country.

Not only do we have our own souls to save, but we have a great country to protect from the fate which has overtaken other civilizations just as strong as ours.

III. AMERICA NEEDS A HIGHER, NOBLER AND A MORE SINCERE FAITH IN GOD

"Righteousness exalteth a nation: but sin is a reproach to any people."—Prov. 14:34.

What we are as a nation we owe to our underlying faith in God: the Pilgrims at Plymouth Rock on their knees; Washington at Valley Forge praying for guidance and strength in the crisis of battle; Lincoln calling the country to national repentance in the midst of civil conflict. These are memorable portraits of our basic faith in God as a nation. If we have any success as a nation, we must attribute the glory, the honor and the praise to a benevolent God who has guided, with omnipotent hand, the course and destiny of our fair land.

In most of our wars, many of our greatest generals were professed Christians, and their decisions and strategy were mingled with sincere prayer and dependence upon Almighty God. It is significant that our enemies, as far as I know, could not boast of one Christian general in their military personnel.

Japan with her war lords and Germany with her atheistic Nazi leaders did not have one military commander who sought the wisdom of God in their military endeavors. Today, as far as I know, none of our enemies are Christians.

Could any fair individual say the prayers offered by devoted mothers and by the churches all over America had nothing to do in bringing about victory for our armed forces? Suffice it to say, the enemy forces, which refused to honor God by seeking His wisdom through prayer, went down into bitter defeat and their systems vanished into oblivion as all civilizations have which left God out of their program.

Abraham Lincoln struck a keynote when he said, "The important thing is not that we have God on our side, but that we make sure we are on His side."

Faith in God often becomes the balance of power when two matched forces are joined in combat; or, more often, the victory often goes to inferior forces when God's power and blessing are upon their efforts. As Moses said—"How should one chase a thousand, and two put ten thousand to flight, except their Rock had sold them, and the Lord had shut them up?" (Deut. 32:30).

When as a lad David dared to face the giant Goliath, he trusted not in swords and staves but in the Lord. He faced the towering giant of the Philistines undaunted, unafraid and said,

"Thou comest to me with a sword, and with a spear, and with a shield: but I come to thee in the name of the Lord of hosts, the God of the armies of Israel, whom thou hast defied. This day will the Lord deliver thee into mine hand; and I will smite thee, and take thine head from thee; and I will give the carcasses of the host of the Philistines this day unto the fowls of the air, and to the wild beasts of the earth; that all the earth may know that there is a God in Israel."—I Sam. 17:45,46.

We need to know as a nation that adequate equipment is insufficient to win a war. Germany had superior planes, tanks and men, but they lost the last war. We must not become smug and complacent. The atomic bomb, without the blessing of God upon our nation, could never win a war.

The most potent weapon in existence is the inward conviction that we are on God's side and that our cause is just and right. We not only need a greater faith in God as a nation but we, as individuals, need to know God in a personal Christian experience.

Lieutenant Whitaker, speaking of his experience, said,

> At forty years of age, I had never been inside a church for any reason whatsoever; but out there on a raft in the middle of the Pacific I met God. I heard Bill Cherry pray, and a rain cloud that had passed us turned around and came back over us and drenched us with water when we were about to die of thirst. It was there I saw God and learned to say, "I believe."

These words are from a hardened military man who found God the hard way. Afterwards, he traveled throughout the land telling the marvelous story of how he met God.

Many of us will never have the unique experience of meeting God under those unusual circumstances, but we can know Him nevertheless.

We can prove His adequacy in the crucible of human experience and know that He is the Christ of every crisis. We can learn to say with Paul, "I know whom I have believed, and am persuaded that he is able to keep that which I have committed unto him against that day" (II Tim. 1:12).

I would rather the citizens of our beloved America should know Christ personally than for America to have the greatest military might in the world. I would rather have it said that we are a people who love God and worship Him than for America to have the security of the atomic bomb. I would rather that Americans should be reverent and humble in their attitude toward Jesus, the Son of God, than to have the rest of the world acclaim us as the mightiest of the nations.

I want to close in the spirit of that touching little poem, "I MET THE MASTER."

> I had walked life's way with an easy tread,
> Had followed where comforts and pleasure led;
> And then one day in a quiet place
> I met the Master, face to face.
>
> With station and rank and wealth for a goal;
> Much thought for the body, but none for the soul;
> I had thought to win in life's mad race,
> When I met the Master, face to face.
>
> I met Him and knew Him and blushed to see
> That eyes full of sorrow were turned on me;
> And I faltered and fell at His feet that day,
> While all my castles melted away—
>
> Melted and vanished, and in their place
> I saw nought else but the Master's face;

And I cried aloud, "Oh, make me meet
To follow the steps of Thy wounded feet."

And now my thoughts are for the souls of men;
I've lost my life, to find it again,
E'er since that day in a quiet place
I met the Master, face to face.

—Author Unknown

(From *30 Years of Plowing, Planting and Watering*—Life Story of B. R. Lakin, by Wm. K. McComas)

MELVIN MUNN
1916-

ABOUT THE MAN:

Melvin Munn was first an announcer for a Dallas CBS radio affiliate, and in 1949 the owners added television. Mr. Munn was a very popular commentator, plain and pointed—like Paul Harvey, for example.

His Life Line *Freedom Talk* 4-page leaflet was his TV talks in printed form. Life Line was "chartered as a non-denominational, religious organization, dedicated to the preservation of American Freedoms through an informed public."

Before they were discontinued, THE SWORD OF THE LORD printed many of Munn's pertinent articles from this fact-packed newspaper, such as "Here Is a Good Four-Letter Word" / "God and Drunkenness" / "The Mother-in-Law" / "Joe Forgets the Pledge" / "Something's Rotten in Denmark" / "Don't Abolish Capital Punishment" / "Abortion Craze" / "Great Men Praise the Bible" / "Who Gives This Child?"

He is a Christian, and writes on many religious subjects. He is also a loyal American who isn't afraid to shoot straight at drugs, one-world government, inflation, gun control, welfare, school textbooks, United Nations, etc.

We need many more Melvin Munns!

IV.

Our Freedom Ideals

MELVIN MUNN, Commentator
Dallas, Texas

Talk given in 1970.

July 4, 1976, closed out 200 years of our national history. Our ancestors declared for freedom. Their descendants are still developing our ideals of freedom.

We believe in—

God, as each man understands Him; the importance of the individual; the freedom of the individual; the profit motive; private ownership of property; the dignity of work; in government as protector, not as provider.

When free men seek to alter, cancel out or destroy any foundation principle upon which their freedom has been built and their liberty purchased, it is imperative that they, and all of us, carefully study what they would abandon.

It is beyond reasonable question that the vast majority of American citizens today place most of their faith in this nation in the great ideals which the people have adopted.

Together, let us review our foundation principles:

We believe in God, as each man understands Him. This is the central ideal, the taproot of America's growth, abundance and preeminence. All other basic elements of our nation's ideological heritage spring from this one central majority thought.

Most of that majority believe in God the Father Almighty as revealed in the Holy Bible. But the genius of America's early planning was that civil authorities made no attempt to use the power of law to force any citizen to believe in any god or any particular form of God.

Vast multitudes of people in Asia and Africa have contrasting beliefs in God as the result of sacred writings from various religions. The ancient books of Hinduism, the Vedas, Buddhism's one hundred volumes of one thousand pages each, the Analects of Confucianism and Islam's Koran have directed the varying ways in which these people understand God.

In the United States most citizens understand God as the person's conscience dictates, based on the single book, our Holy Bible.

No man or men can alter history in such a way as to remove God from the founding principles of our land. Dictators could take it out of textbooks, prohibit any worship of God and punish any who publicly mentioned God's name, but they can't change fact.

God was prominent in the prayerful preparation of the Declaration of Independence. God was in the minds and hearts of those who later attended the Constitutional Convention where Benjamin Franklin said, *"I have lived, Sir, a long time, and the longer I live, the more convincing proofs I see of this truth—that God governs in the affairs of men."*

President John Adams later affirmed that *"the general Principles, on which the Fathers achieved independence,"* are the *"general Principles of Christianity and the general Principles of English and American Liberty."*

Those before us believed in God; we believe in God, just as those before us trusted in Him and just as we trust Him. With our acceptance and understanding of God as our Creator, citizens of the United States, in the main, have accepted Locke's concept of the divine rights of man—of every man. Our founding ideals are those God-given rights.

We believe in the importance of the individual. Every animal, except man, has to adjust to its environment. Man alone constantly alters his environment. But always remember that whatever change man makes collectively has to first begin as an idea in the mind of some single individual.

Powerful among our ideals of freedom is this thought that the individual person is sacred, important and a creature of potential dignity.

The great difference between man and all other animal life on earth dramatizes the obvious fact that man is different. That difference is his link with the Infinite, with universality, with time eternal and with factors and elements not available to any other living thing on earth.

There is no valid, logical or provable explanation for this uniqueness except for the knowledge that there is a divine Creator, that all men are created in His image and that each man has a spark of the Creator in his own life.

Every living human being is a little creator endowed by God with the capacity for abstract thought and for conceiving new things and new processes. Each human being has the power to reason, to hold opinions, to judge, to recollect and reflect, to purpose, to intend and to work out answers and solutions. Thus all men are endowed by God with creative and inventive powers which are now known to be absolute requisites for human progress. Without these powers there would be no innovation, no invention, no planned improvement.

Besides, the "laws of nature and of nature's God" clearly demonstrate that man can achieve true fulfillment only through the use of his inner powers and talents. There would be no progress if each man's creative and inventive endowments were the same as every other man's.

Some people want to study history; others like agriculture, athletics, mining, teaching, the ministry, medicine or any one of an endless variety of specializations and combinations of human endeavor. Only a free individual can progress in his own particular way, and society moves much more efficiently and productively when it is the beneficiary of millions of individual efforts—far more than it ever could by force-directed uniform action in one direction by the millions.

Thomas Jefferson caught the spirit of freedom for the individual when he wrote: *"We hold these truths to be self-evident, that all men. . . are endowed by their Creator with certain unalienable rights."* He stressed the vital value of the individual by saying that *"governments are instituted among men"* so that these natural rights can be secure as civil rights.

We believe in the freedom of the individual. Even the casual mind would have to be impressed with the high rating given to freedom and liberty by those who first organized this nation. The freedom they envisioned has expressed itself in countless ways and manifests itself in the sizable reservoir of liberty that still remains with us. The value of freedom for the individual is never so dramatically impressed upon the thinking man's mind as when he begins to consider how much freedom he has lost even in this country.

Daniel Webster in a speech on June 3, 1834, warned, *"God grants liberty only to those who love it, and are always ready to guard and defend it."*

Woodrow Wilson cautioned: *"The history of liberty is a history of the limitation of governmental power, not the increase of it. When we resist concentration of power, we are resisting the processes of death, because concentration of power is what always precedes the destruction of human liberties."*

Destiny rules that freedom has its major parts in a unit of one. The nearer we can come to providing maximum freedom under the rules of moral and legal law for the individual, the closer we come to perpetuating freedom for the nation.

July 4, 1776, was the birth date of the United States of America. It is the only nation with a known birthday. July, 1976, was the anniversary month of our 200th birthday as a nation.

If what I say here is very familiar to you, there is no reason for surprise, for I am simply restating the principal ideals upon which this nation and her people have built, grown, served and succeeded through two centuries without a break in her governmental processes.

We believe in the profit motive. With a slight paraphrasing of the Bible, let me raise the question, "For what does it profit a man to gain the whole world, and forfeit his life?" Implicit in the response to that question will be two truths:

1. It is the nature of man to be motivated by what he believes will profit him.

2. Preoccupation with materialism to the exclusion of moral and spiritual values produces no reward that lasts.

The phrase "profit motive" is simply another way of saying hope of rewards. It is perfectly natural for man to choose to do things he feels will benefit or profit him.

Private enterprise Americans who develop, manufacture and improve products do so in the hope of compensation for initiative, imagination, work and financial risk.

Young people who spend years of their lives and much money on an education do so hoping to increase their opportunities and earning power and to be able to contribute the maximum back to society at large. Housewives shop for bargains, employees add imagination to their work, scientists search for new physical truths, and inventors produce dramatic tools, devices and instruments for many people to use. All this they do in the hope of reward.

You can be done with the idea that our system calls for total selfishness, for I hold that inner rewards to successful men almost always outweigh any material gain they may secure. Thus the profit motive— the hope of reward—is an American ideal where man is enriched by giving of himself and rewarded for his honesty and effort.

We believe in private ownership of property. As far back as October 14, 1774, the Declaration and Resolves of the First Continental Congress stated, *"by the immutable laws of nature, they (the colonists) are entitled to life, liberty, and property."* To deny individuals the right to own property interferes with their lives, violates their liberty, weakens their hope of reward and jeopardizes the foundations of freedom.

James Madison wrote: *"Government is instituted to protect property of every sort."* Property of every sort includes time, inner emotions, jobs—indeed, take away a man's property and nothing is left but a walking shell.

We believe in the dignity of work. The advantages of work are seen in the fact that the needs and wants of mankind cannot be satisfied without work. There is no other way of meeting the demands of men.

We believe in government as protector, not as provider. Those who organized the United States of America placed definite limits on the *"just powers"* of governments by chaining those powers to the will of the people. Only by the consent of those who are to be governed are governments to be established and maintained for free men.

These ideals make it clear that every individual has a divine right to his life, his liberty and his property. That divine right is not to be transgressed by law, by government or by tyrants.

Let the people daily reaffirm their faith in the basic ideals of freedom, and most American ills will soon be cured.

JOHN R. RICE
1895-1980

ABOUT THE MAN:

Preacher . . . evangelist . . . revivalist . . . editor . . . counselor to thousands . . . friend to millions—that was Dr. John R. Rice, whose accomplishments were nothing short of miraculous. Known as "America's Dean of Evangelists," Dr. Rice made a mighty impact upon the nation's religious life for some sixty years, in great citywide campaigns and in Sword of the Lord Conferences.

At age nine, after hearing a sermon on "The Prodigal Son," John went forward to claim Christ as Saviour. In 1916, with only $9.35 in his pocket, he rode off on his cowpony toward Decatur Baptist College. He was now on the road to becoming a world-renowned evangelist, although he was then totally unaware of God's will for his life.

There was many a twist and turn before Rice rode through the open door into full-time preaching—the army, marriage, graduate work, more seminary, assistant pastor, pastor—then FINALLY, where God planned to use him most—in full-time evangelism.

Dr. Rice and his miniistry were always colorful (born in Cooke county, in Texas, December 11, 1895, and often called "Will Rogers of the Pulpit" because of their likeness and mannerisms)—and controversial. CONTROVERSIAL—and correctly so—because of his intense stand against modernism and infidelity and his fight for the Fundamentals.

Dr. Rice lived and died a man of convictions—intense convictions. But, like many other strong fighters for the Faith, Rice was also marked with a sincere spirit of compassion. Those who knew him best knew a man who loved them. In preaching, in prayer, and in personal life, Rice wept over sinners and with saints. But there is more . . .

Less than seventy-one hours before the dawning of 1981, one of the most prolific pens in all Christendom was stilled. Dr. John R. Rice left behind a legacy in writing of more than 200 titles, with a combined circulation of over 61 million copies. And through October of 1981, a total of 24,058 precious souls reported trusting Christ through his ministries, not counting those saved in his crusades nor in foreign countries where his literature has been translated.

And who but God knows the influence of THE SWORD OF THE LORD magazine which he started and edited for forty-six years.

And while "Twentieth Century's Mightiest Pen"—and man—has been stilled, thank God, the fruit remains! Though dead, he continues to speak.

V.

"Blessed Is the Nation Whose God Is the Lord . . ."

JOHN R. RICE

"Blessed is the nation whose God is the Lord; and the people whom he hath chosen for his own inheritance."—Ps. 33:12.

"Righteousness exalteth a nation: but sin is a reproach to any people."—Prov. 14:34.

The Scripture does not say that a nation to be blessed must have every person converted. It does not even say that a majority of the nation must be born-again Christians. It says, 'Blessed is the nation who recognizes the Lord God as their God.'

When the people of Israel were brought out of Egypt and led to the land of promise, and later when they were blessed under the kingdom of David and his son—they were not all Christians. Not all observed the moral standards of the law. But God was the God of Israel, and Israel was recognized as His people. So in some sense, America can claim that the Lord God of the Bible is our God. And America ought to and can be a nation of God-fearing people, therefore, a blessed nation.

The Bible makes it clear that God deals with nations as well as with individuals. He chose Jacob to be the father of the nation Israel. He chose for them their land, the time of their possession and their line of kings through whom the Saviour was to come. He gave them their laws, raised up their prophets and kings.

God dealt with the Amorites as a people; and when their iniquity was full, He had Israel take their land.

God remembered the long, continued sin of the Amalekites, so He pronounced judgment upon them. As a nation they were to be destroyed—men, women and children—as He commanded King Saul to do.

God brought judgment on Egypt as a nation because of her oppression of Israel.

He clearly caused the fall of Babylon because of Babylon's sins, and warned Belshazzar by the writing on the wall, interpreted by Daniel (Dan. 5).

God foretold the fall of Tyre and Sidon because of their sins.

God deals with nations as with individuals.

Romans 13:1 tells us that "the powers that be are ordained of God." Nebuchadnezzar, the mighty king of Babylon, the first world emperor, became proud and haughty over his successes. So God gave him a vision, which Daniel interpreted:

"...they shall drive thee from men, and thy dwelling shall be with the beasts of the field, and they shall make thee to eat grass as oxen, and they shall wet thee with the dew of heaven, and seven times shall pass over thee, till thou know that the most High ruleth in the kingdom of men, and giveth it to whomsoever he will."—Dan. 4:25.

Again and again Nebuchadnezzar had been reminded that God had given the Jews into his hands for punishment and that God had allowed him to be the king of Babylon.

God had dealt with Necho, king of Egypt, and commanded him to come "to fight against Charchemish by Euphrates." Necho told King Josiah of Judah:

"I come not against thee this day, but against the house wherewith I have war: for God commanded me to make haste: forbear thee from meddling with God, who is with me, that he destroy thee not."—II Chron. 35:21.

Not heeding the warning, God allowed Josiah to be killed.

God put it in the heart of Cyrus, king of Persia, to command the Jews to go back to Jerusalem to build the Temple again (II Chron. 36:23).

God gave through Daniel to Nebuchadnezzar the outline of the world empires (Dan., chapt. 2 and 7), even the empires of Babylon, Media-Persia, Greece and Rome, then the kingdoms that would come out of Rome, and at last the rise of the Antichrist and his kingdom—then the kingdom of Christ on earth.

Surely the nations are in the hand of God, and He deals with nations as entities and not only with individuals.

So—"Blessed is the nation whose God is the Lord." America will give an account to God. America will be dealt with as a nation, punished for her sins or protected for her faithfulness to certain great principles God has given.

I. AMERICA HAS A GREAT CHRISTIAN HERITAGE

What nation is there in all the world which has had such Christian beginnings as had America!

1. The American Colonies Were Founded Primarily for Religious Ends

After fleeing from England to Holland, the Pilgrims came to America, seeking religious liberty. After a long voyage in a small sailing ship, 102 people landed in America. On the 11th of November, 1620, in Provincetown, they met and went into The Mayflower Compact which said:

> In the name of God, Amen.
> We whose names are underwritten, loyal subjects of our dread sovereign lord, King James, by Grace of God, of Great Britain, France, and Ireland king, Defender of the Faith, and so forth, having undertaken, for the Glory of God and advancement of the Christian Faith, and honor of our King and Country, a voyage to plant the first colony in the northern parts of Virginia, do by this document solemnly and mutually in the presence of God and one another, covenant and combine ourselves together into a civil body politic, for our better ordering and preservation and furtherance of the ends aforesaid; and by virtue of this document enact, constitute and frame such just and equal laws, ordinances, acts, constitutions and offices, from time to time, as shall be thought right for the general good of the colony, unto which we promise all due submission and obedience. In witness we have hereunder subscribed our names at Cape Cod the eleventh of November, in the eighteenth year of the reign of our sovereign lord, King James.
>
> 1620 A.D.

Remember that this Compact was made "In the name of God, Amen." They had undertaken "for the Glory of God and advancement of the Christian Faith, and honor of our King and Country, a voyage to plant the first colony in the northern parts of Virginia." They signed the document, "Solemnly and mutually in the presence of God."

It is noteworthy that the French explorers in Canada and the Spanish explorers in Latin America came for wealth and conquest. Despite the work of the Spanish missions, the adventurers sought for gold, turned to piracy, intermarried with the natives. But the stock that peopled the original thirteen colonies in America came primarily as religious, industrious, Bible-believing people who not only sought economic opportunity but religious as well as political freedom.

In 1630 the colonists in the New England Federation signed this Compact:

> We all have come into these parts of America with one and the same end; namely, to advance the Kingdom of the Lord Jesus Christ.

Speaking in the National Presbyterian Church in Washington, Louis H. Evans said:

> Our history has been inseparable from Christianity. The Pilgrims landed in Plymouth in the name of Christ. The Huguenots came here in the name of God. William Penn settled Pennsylvania in the name of the Nazarene, and the padres landed on the shores of California with crucifixes in their hands. The kiss of God has been upon our face as we have grown from national babyhood to what we trust is but our young manhood.

The great American and statesman, Daniel Webster, well said:

> Lastly, our ancestors established their system of government on morality and religious sentiment. Moral habits, they believed, cannot safely be trusted on any other foundation than religious principle, nor any government be secure which is not supported by moral habits. Living under the heavenly light of revelation, they hoped to find all the social dispositions, all the duties which men owe to each other and to society, enforced and performed. Whatever makes men good Christians, makes them good citizens. . . .

He also penned:

> Finally, let us not forget the religious character of our origin. Our fathers were brought hither by their high veneration for the Christian religion. They journeyed by its light and labored in its hope. They sought to incorporate its principles with the elements of their society and to diffuse its influence through all their institutions, civil, political or literary.
>
> Let us cherish these sentiments and extend this influence still more widely; in the full conviction that that is the happiest society which partakes in the highest degree of the mild and peaceful spirit of Christianity.

It was hard for the colonists, with the world not yet accustomed to the idea of religious freedom, to allow the others the same religious freedom which they sought for themselves. So Roger Williams went in to establish the colony of Rhode Island. Catholics sought freedom from persecution in Maryland and allowed freedom to others. William Penn and Quakers settled Pennsylvania. In Virginia, the state church idea was strong. Baptists were at first persecuted for preaching the Gospel, but Patrick Henry defended nobly two Baptist preachers so charged. George Washington lent his influence and in the Bill of Rights, Article Three declared that in America there would be no establishment of religion and no hindrance of religious freedom.

2. The American Government Was Founded on the Basic Understanding That the God of the Bible Is the True God; That Our Rights and Liberties Are Given by God; That the Nation Must Depend on God for Prosperity and Blessing and Must Answer to God for Our Sins

The Declaration of Independence begins:

> When in the course of human events, it becomes necessary for one people to dissolve the political bands which have connected them with another, and to assume among the powers of the earth, the separate and equal station to which the laws of nature and of nature's God entitle them . . . .

Here is recognized "the laws of nature" as being from God, and the founders of our country acknowledge their responsibility to "the laws of God."

The second sentence reads:

> We hold these truths to be self-evident, that all men are created equal, that they are endowed by their Creator with certain unalienable rights . . . .

Men are "created." They did not evolve from animals. They are the work of a "Creator," and that Creator—God—endowed men with "certain unalienable rights." That is another way of saying what the national hymn says,

> **Our father's God! to Thee,**
> **Author of liberty,**
> **To Thee we sing.**

In declaring their independence from Great Britain, the representatives of the United States of America in conclusion said,

> We, therefore, the representatives of the United States of America,

in general congress, assembled, appealing to the Supreme Judge of
the world for the rectitude of our intentions. . . .

—that is, they were signing this Declaration of Independence in the fear
of God, looking to Him for the righteousness of their action and to reward
it. And they solemnly published and declared,

> These United Colonies are, and of Right ought to be, free and in-
> dependent states.

". . . of right ought to be," and in the Declaration of Independence,
as it is engraved on copper and framed in my office, the word "Right"
is spelled with a capital R. For the declarers who signed their names
meant that God Himself who had created them had established the principles that made them properly free and independent.

As earnestly as any congregation organizing itself as a local church
may declare that the organization is to be founded, they believe, in accordance with the will of God, so these signers of the Declaration of
Independence claimed that God was with them, and He was their
Creator and their rights they received from God, and thus that it was
God's will that the American States become independent under the circumstances. Actually, the Christian religion was regarded as basic in
the founding of the United States as a separate nation.

When the Continental Congress took up the matter of forming a single
nation of the separate colonies, each with its own laws, its own money,
taxes, import duties, they argued and worked for long weeks seeking
some plan on which they could agree. At last Benjamin Franklin stood
up and said:

> I have lived, sir, a long time; and the longer I live, the more con-
> vincing proofs I see of this truth, that God governs in the affairs of
> men. If a sparrow cannot fall to the ground without His notice, is it
> probable that an empire can rise without His aid? We have been
> assured, sir, in the Sacred Writings that "except the Lord build the
> house, they labor in vain that build it." I firmly believe this; and I also
> believe that without His concurring aid we shall succeed in this political
> building no better than the builders of Babel.

The delegates agreed and then stopped for fervent prayer. The difficulty seemed soon to dissolve, and out of their meeting grew that great
historic Constitution of the United States, probably the most important
political document ever written.

So the colonies became "one nation under God." It would be foolish to contend that America was not founded with the help of God or that our founders did not claim that help.

So in the new nation pains were taken to nurture the Christian religion (not denominations, not an established church) and to regularly recognize God in our government. This was manifested in several ways.

1. Elected men were to be sworn into office by solemn oaths that recognized God as witness. And for Quakers and others who, for religious convictions, felt not free to use an oath, they were allowed to "solemnly affirm" with the same implications. Many have even questioned whether an atheist could constitutionally take that oath. And the oath is required for every witness in every court. It has been the unwritten law that every President of the United States must take the oath of office upon a Bible.

2. It is provided that there should be a chaplain both for the United States Senate and House of Representatives to open each session of either of these two Houses of Congress with prayer.

Our founders meant that Congress should seek the wisdom of God in lawmaking activities and that every legislative hall should be a house of prayer. It normally followed that, in the army and navy and now in the marines and air force, there should be chaplains in the services to pray and warn and counsel and comfort. Our founders expected that when we of necessity went to battle, we would pray for God to prosper our armies and deliver our country from enemies.

3. It was provided that Christian institutions (churches and Christian schools) should be tax-free, to encourage these desirable institutions for the welfare of our country.

4. On every American coin is the motto, IN GOD WE TRUST; so every silver dollar, half dollar, quarter, dime, nickel or penny says that America was intended by the founders to be a God-fearing nation, even a Christian nation.

5. In 1789 Congress passed the Bill of Rights, and ten of the proposed amendments to the Constitution were adopted by the States. Article 3 reads,

> Congress shall make no law respecting an establishment of religion or prohibiting the free exercise thereof, or abridging the freedom of speech, or of the press, or of the right of the people peaceably to assemble and to petition the government for redress of grievances.

Note carefully that the government is not neutral on the matter of religion. It is not against religion, but against the establishment of an official state religion, since that would be unfair to others. It specially prohibits any abridgment of the right of people to worship, to assemble for worship and to speak or preach or publish religion. It is not to forbid prayer in the schools, but to see that nobody shall be coerced to pray or to pray a certain way or forbidden to pray. It is not to forbid the use of the Bible in the schoolroom, but to see that nobody opposes the Bible or coerces people to read the Bible. It is for religious freedom and thus favoring the Christian religion.

3. The Noblest and Most Influential American Leaders Have Favored the Christian Religion

I do not mean that every one of the noble men who took active part in founding or in leading this nation has been a born-again Christian. Some we think were not; some others we do not know.

The father of his country, General George Washington, was a devout Christian. How nobly he led that little band, poorly fed, poorly clothed and discouraged men, in the Continental army! And in the long winter in Valley Forge, we are told that George Washington went alone to kneel in the snow and pray for God's blessing on the little army. We may be sure that God did bless the leadership of General Washington and did answer the prayer of good men in giving the colonies freedom from Great Britain.

It is said that a gentleman from South Carolina visited New York where the Continental Congress was meeting and told a friend, "I should like to see General Washington. How may I distinguish him in the meeting?" The friend replied, "General Washington will be the tall man who kneels when the Continental Congress stops for prayer."

The Hebrew Congregation in Newport, Rhode Island, wrote a letter to President Washington. He replied that, "Happily the government of the United States gives to bigotry no sanction, to persecution, no assistance . . . ." And he closed it with these words: "May the Father of all mercies scatter light and not darkness on our paths, and make us all in our several vocations useful here, and in His own due time and way everlastingly happy." Was not that a noble and Christian sentiment?

Tom Paine had written useful tracts for liberty to stir the people for the Revolutionary War. But being an infidel, when he returned to America from imprisonment in France, he was poorly received, given no place in the new government and retired to the little farm given him where he spent his last days in filth and drunkenness. The early leaders of America were not for atheism, but for the Bible and for God.

Our national anthem, "The Star-Spangled Banner," was written during the War of 1812 by Francis Scott Key. One verse says:

Blest with victory and peace, may the Heav'n-rescued land
Praise the Power that hath made and preserved us a nation!
Then conquer we must, when our cause it is just,
And this be our motto, "In God is our Trust."

"America," our national hymn, recognizes God as the God of America:

Our fathers' God! to Thee,
Author of liberty,
To thee we sing:
Long may our land be bright
With freedom's holy light;
Protect us by Thy might,
Great God, our King.

The national and official acceptance of these sentiments means that the best leadership has intended for America to be Christian in spirit and in dependence on God.

The first book printed in America was *"The Whole Books of Psalms, Faithfully Translated into English Metre,"* in 1640 in the Bay State, Massachusetts.

Thomas Jefferson wrote and published in 1774 a pamphlet, *A Summary of the Rights of British America,* that is, the colonies in which he said, "The God who gave us life gave us liberty at the same time."

Time would fail me to tell of the statements of Samuel Adams and John Adams, of Daniel Webster, of Ulysses S. Grant, of Robert E. Lee, of Theodore Roosevelt, of Woodrow Wilson and nearly every President and great leader America has ever known, showing a devotion to the Bible. Even our profane President, Harry Truman, humbly asked for prayer at his inauguration.

At his inauguration, President Eisenhower read this prayer which he himself had written:

Almighty God, as we stand here at this moment, my future associates in the executive branch of the government join me in beseeching that Thou would make full and complete our dedication to the service of the people in this throng and their fellow citizens everywhere.

Give us, we pray, the power to discern right from wrong.

He prayed for all the people that ". . . all may work for the good of our beloved country and Thy glory. Amen."

Every cabinet meeting, the Governors' conference at the White House, and other such important meetings under President Eisenhower were opened with prayer.

At his inauguration President Lyndon B. Johnson declared his dependence on God.

I well remember how as a soldier during World War I, I received a little Testament with an earnest plea by President Woodrow Wilson that we trust Christ as Saviour and live for Him.

General Douglas MacArthur, the greatest hero of World War II, in his address, "Where I Stand," said:

> Our need for patriotic fervor and religious devotion was never more impelling. There can be no compromise with atheistic communism— no half-way in the preservation of freedom and religion. It must be all or nothing.
>
> * * * * *
>
> It is an infallible reminder that our greatest hope and faith rests upon two mighty symbols—the Cross and the Flag. . . .
>
> * * * * *
>
> We must unite in the high purpose that the liberties etched upon the design of our life be unimpaired and that we maintain the moral courage and spiritual leadership to preserve inviolate that mighty bulwark of all freedom, our Christian faith.

General MacArthur requested American churches to send thousands of missionaries to Japan.

On the train platform about to leave Springfield, Illinois, tall, gaunt, President-elect Lincoln said to his fellow townsmen:

> I leave now, not knowing when, or whether ever, I shall return, with a task before me greater than that which rested on the shoulders of Washington.
> Without the assistance of the Divine Being, who ever attended him, I cannot succeed. With that assistance I cannot fail. Trusting in Him who can go with me, and remain with you and be everywhere for good, let us confidently hope that all will be well.

Before the presidency, Lincoln was God-fearing, seeking, but doubtful. In the presidency, he matured and came reassured to a definite faith in God and in Christ.

It has been a national custom for the President to proclaim an annual day of Thanksgiving. Thus through the years America has officially taken the position that the Lord God is our God, that America at least claims to be, and the best in America all hope to be, a Christian America.

II. GOD HAS BLESSED AMERICA BEYOND OTHER NATIONS

Our text, Psalm 33:12, says, "Blessed is the nation whose God is the Lord." Surely the smile of God has been upon the United States more than on any other contemporary nation.

America has riches beyond other nations. The blacks of America complain of their "underprivileged" state, but actually, as President Hoover reminded us, "Negroes in America have more cars than everybody together in Soviet Russia." Today (1975) Americans have 68 million automobiles, 89 million telephones, 55 million television sets, 7.7 million pleasure boats. They spend money at an annual rate of $419 billion, according to *Newsweek* (June 14, 1965). And again *Newsweek* says,

> Besides loading up on material goods, Americans are pampering themselves with the pleasant things of life as never before. Last year they spent $774 million on musical instruments and helped support more music teachers (400,000) than there are people in Luxembourg.

People are buying big cars, most often have two cars to a family, air-conditioning in cars and homes and wall-to-wall carpeting and color TV—to name a few. People are going on expensive vacations, staying at luxurious motels, patronizing expensive restaurants.

Materially, America is rich as no other nation in the world has been rich. The poorest people in America expect to have a car, an electric refrigerator and a television.

America has been greatly blessed in other matters. We do not have the oppressive dictation of a state church. We can travel from state to state without registering with police, quit a job or change jobs without government permission, go to church or stay at home, and vote for whom we please.

If David was right to say, "Bless the Lord, O my soul: and all that is within me, bless his holy name. Bless the Lord, O my soul, and forget not all his benefits" (Ps. 103:1,2), surely Americans should thank God for material and spiritual blessings.

Will you remember that when this is written, in India, Mexico and in many other nations, new missionaries are refused admittance? That in Israel missionary work is not allowed and a man recently lost his citizenship by leaving the Jewish religion to become a Catholic? That in England, Baptists, Methodists and others not in the Anglican church are taxed to support the state church, as are other church groups in Spain, in Scandinavian countries and in Germany and South American countries? That in England the Baptist congregation cannot call its building a "church," but must call it a "chapel," because it is not the state church?

How wonderful is the freedom of America!

Although the church membership (a majority in America are aligned with some church or religion) does not consist necessarily of born-again Christians, and does not involve in most cases perhaps either a regenerated heart or a transformed life, yet America has more churches, sings more hymns and gospel songs, has more religious opportunity than anywhere in the world.

And how God has protected America in this war-torn world! By God's mercy we have never fought a war of aggression. We went into World War I and World War II to oppose tyranny and rescue others from oppression, as well as to retain our own nation's integrity. We have not sought colonies. We freed Cuba. We freed the Philippine Islands. We have given away billions of dollars to help poor countries, often to countries made poor by their own strife and ignorance and sin, and just as often when the help was unappreciated.

I do not endorse the Marshall Plan nor much of the foreign aid program, but at least one can say that the national policy of America has been unselfish and altruistic. Our soft hearts sometimes indicate also soft heads, but what a blessing of God that the American people have had a heart for the poor, the ignorant and the oppressed everywhere!

God has delivered us from the attackers, from Germany's U-Boats and from Japanese aggression. Compared with England, France, Belgium, Germany, Italy, Japan, Russia, China, Korea, how little America has suffered from wars!

Americans everywhere ought to devoutly thank God for His blessings. And we can surely say about America, "Blessed is the nation whose God is the Lord; and the people whom he hath chosen for his own inheritance."

III. AMERICA IS DRIFTING FROM GOD

America has more church members now than it ever had. And counting modernists, false cults, Catholics, Mormons, Unitarians and all, a little over half of the American people belong to some religious organization. But it is only fair to say that only a fraction of this number are born-again Christians or those who hold to the historic Christian faith. Of course, modernists and such liberals do not believe in the absolute deity of Christ nor the infallible inspiration of the Bible. Neither do Mormons, Christian Scientists, Unitarians nor Jehovah's Witnesses.

And so the impact of Christianity on America is relatively less than it has been in former times.

1. Officially and Governmentally America Is Not Nearly So Christian as Our Founding Fathers Anticipated

Once churches, Christian colleges and seminaries and religious magazines were counted a great asset to the welfare of America. Now there is a persistent effort by left-wing and religious liberals to cancel its tax-free status if a magazine or institution stresses too hard against liquor or communism or modernists.

Once in our schools people learned to read from the Bible. The famous McGuffey Readers were based upon the morality of the Bible and often referred to the Bible. Now a student may graduate from high school or college and never see a Bible nor learn a single quotation from the Bible.

The Supreme Court, acting on a suit brought by an atheist, declared unconstitutional the prayer prepared by the education council in New York State. And the general tendency has been to forbid prayer of any kind in the schoolroom, although quite obviously that was far from the intention and practice of our Founding Fathers.

In my boyhood we memorized little prayers in the first and second grade. It was customary over most of America to have ministers come and speak to schools. In my early ministry, I have often seen the schools dismiss for one hour daily to attend the weekday revival services. I was often invited to speak in high schools and colleges, simply to preach the Gospel. Once when I was engaged in revival services in the Second Presbyterian Church in Chattanooga, Tennessee, I was invited to speak in every high school in the city and in the principal grade schools, both white and colored, and was gladly received. The only people offended were those involved in the few elementary schools where I could not come for lack of time. But now, led by the liberal Supreme Court, the tendency is to make God neutral toward religion instead of favorable to Christianity, as our Founding Fathers intended. Governmentally, America is drifting away from God.

In World War I, principal evangelistic preachers in America came to the army camps to preach, and hundreds were converted. They were usually brought in by the chaplains. Dr. George W. Truett, famous Southern Baptist preacher, went to Europe under the auspices of the Y.M.C.A. and preached to multiplied thousands of soldiers.

But the pattern has changed. The Y.M.C.A. itself is now not evangelistic and not necessarily Christian. The chaplains in the armed services are usually liberals. Sometimes they smoke and drink. They preach only in the small chapels. The same men usually buy the beer for the parties and chaperone the dances. No more is there a great breaking out of revival and soul winning in the army camps, as was true in World War I, and as was true in the Civil War when D. L. Moody and the Christian Commission went to all the Union armies for soul winning, and as General Stonewall Jackson and Robert E. Lee emphasized soul winning and prayer meetings in the Confederate armies. Governmentally, America has drifted far from God.

God-fearing, decent citizens ought to be alarmed by these recent statistics:

The Census Bureau reveals single men and women living together number more than 2 million [1987];

That 30,000 unborn babies are killed EVERY WEEK by abortion; 125,000 monthly; 1,500,000 yearly in the United States. Worldwide— one million EACH WEEK [1986];

That today over 800,000 unwed girls become pregnant every year [1985];

That half the marriages in the U.S. end in divorce;

That close to 15 million Americans, including 3 million under 18, have severe drinking problems; three out of four teenagers drink [1985];

[We don't have the tragic figure on the use of drugs, but it is enormous];

That 34.2 million crimes were committed in 1986, including rapes, robberies, assaults, thefts [1986].

100 murders a year are committed in public schools and at least 70,000 teachers are assaulted. And we are all aware that homosexuals abound, with the deadly AIDS.

Oh, America is drifting away from God, and the great moral breakdown begins to show its bitter fruit.

3. A Breakdown in Christian Conviction and Spiritual Religion Is Back of Our Drift Away From God

The Supreme Court presses to get the Bible and prayer out of our schools because the Supreme Court represents the socialistic trend in America and its breakdown of convictions. It is supported by the public sentiment.

In a republic like ours, the officials are, directly or indirectly, subject to the people. The President is elected, and he appoints Supreme Court Justices who fit the popular standards. If the Supreme Court is soft on communism, it is because, after long years of New-Deal philosophy, governmental handouts and constant propaganda, the people themselves are also soft on communism. If the Supreme Court is anxious not to offend infidels and atheists by allowing prayer and Bible reading in the schools, then they simply represent the mass of people who do not want to offend Mormons, Moslems, Unitarians and modernists, all of whom are influential in politics and who do not hold to the historic Christian convictions of our Founding Fathers.

And whence comes this horrible breakdown in moral standards in America? Why is sex pressed on the people? Why are movies and magazines more lewd and women less virtuous and men more profane than ever before? Because America, with its tens of millions of church members, has relatively few strong Bible preachers. There is little campaigning among Christians and from the pulpits against the curse of the liquor business, against the commercializing of vice and lewdness by the movies and TV. There is little warning and protest about necking, petting, the looseness of the dance, unchaperoned dates and the shocking percentage of adultery.

Not many preachers preach on sin, on the coming judgment, on an awful Hell for Christ-rejecting sinners. There is not much preaching on "The way of transgressors is hard" (Prov. 13:15) and "Be sure your sin will find you out" (Num. 32:23) and "Be not deceived; God is not mocked: for whatsoever a man soweth, that shall he also reap" (Gal. 6:7).

The pulpit has failed the churches, and the churches have failed America. So the padded church rolls are crowded with the names of the unconverted. And those who have been converted are often worldly themselves and never protest nor break fellowship with others over their sin.

Now preachers who do not believe the Bible pretend to lead in spiritual things! Those who deny all the essentials of the historic Christian faith are made bishops and go to the biggest pulpits and are officers of the National Council of Churches! Now those who trample on the blood of Christ and spit on the Bible are called Christians!

But people who compromise and have small convictions about the Christian religion cannot be trusted to have much conviction about Americanism. Those who are not enemies of sin and Satan and unbelief, will not be enemies of communism and socialism. The drift of America away from God is primarily a religious problem.

IV. AMERICA, PREPARE TO MEET GOD!

God deals with nations as entities, as well as dealing with individuals. In Amos 4:12 God says, "Therefore thus will I do unto thee, O Israel: and because I will do this unto thee, prepare to meet thy God, O Israel."

The Lord reminds Israel that He had warned them again and again with famine; He had withheld the rain; He had smitten their crops with blasting and mildew; He had sent pestilence among them and war, "yet have ye not returned unto me, saith the Lord." Therefore, He warns them, "Prepare to meet thy God, O Israel."

We preach to lost sinners, "Prepare to meet God"; and we do well, for every individual who reads this must meet God in person. But in this life, God also judges nations.

He judged Egypt, bringing the plagues and then destroying Pharaoh and his army in the Red Sea, because of their oppression of Israel.

The Canaanite nations were destroyed after years of God's dealing as they went on with their idolatry. God gave the land to Israel. Israel, after many warnings, was carried into captivity to Babylon; and the Temple was destroyed. Later the Saviour came to the restored remnant of Israel; and when He was rejected and crucified, God let Titus and the Roman army destroy Jerusalem so that not one stone was left on another, and Jews were scattered to all the world!

God brought judgment on Babylon; and when Belshazzar made a feast for a thousand of his lords and drank wine from the holy vessels of the Temple of God, there appeared the fingers of a man's hand, miraculously writing on the plaster of the wall: "Thou art weighed in the balances, and art found wanting." That night Belshazzar died in sudden invasion and Darius the Mede took the kingdom.

God brought disaster on Rome because of her sins; also on Germany and Italy. God is saying to America, "Prepare to meet thy God."

And how are we to prepare to meet God?

1. Back to Fundamental Christianity, the Historic Christian Faith!

Our churches must come back to the Bible if they are to claim the promise of prosperity given in Psalm 1:1-3. There must be a renewed emphasis on the inspiration and authority of the Bible, on the deity of Christ, His virgin birth, His bodily resurrection, His atonement on the cross and the promise of His second coming. There must be a new emphasis on the wages of sin, the certainty of judgment, on Heaven and Hell.

The liberalism of German universities that plunged Europe and the world into two bloody world wars will damn America. Honest Christians should clean the infidels out of the churches or get out themselves.

It is said that once an Irishman mounted a horse with some timidity because of his lack of experience. On that summer day the flies were bad and the horse stomped his hind feet again and again to scatter the flies from his belly. Eventually one foot caught in the stirrup of the saddle. The Irishman was startled. "Begorra," he said, "if you are going to get on, I'm going to get off!"

So a Christian who believes the Bible should make up his mind to take a plain stand against infidelity in the church. He should not associate with it and count it Christian. He should not support it with his money. The preacher who does not believe in the deity and virgin birth and blood atonement of Jesus Christ has no right to the presence of Christians in his congregation nor to their support for his salary. The Ministerial Association that counts an infidel as a Christian simply because he is a pastor and gives Christian recognition to the enemies of Christ and the Bible, is not a fit fellowship for a born-again man of God.

If America is to have the blessing of God in the future as it has had by mercy in the past, then Christians should return to the historic Christian faith. It is still true that "the Bible is the bulwark of our liberties" as General Grant, President Lincoln, Daniel Webster, President Woodrow Wilson, President Theodore Roosevelt and many another great American believed. American greatness is based on the Bible as the very Word of God. The way to God's continued blessing is for those who take the name of Christ to go back to the Bible and to the Christ of the Bible.

And this return to the Bible and Christ must not be only an intellectual involvement. There must be a return to heartfelt religion, to concern over sinners, to a holy devotion to Christ and a brokenhearted seeking after the lost. We need to return to the revival preaching, to the invitation song, to the personal soul winning and house-to-house visitation of New Testament Christianity.

It was no accident that George Whitefield and Jonathan Edwards and Charles G. Finney and A. B. Earle and D. L. Moody and his associates and Sam Jones and Billy Sunday—great soul winners—rose on the American scene. The revival campaign was native to early America, when America could claim the promise of Psalm 33:12: "Blessed is the nation whose God is the Lord; and the people whom he hath chosen for his own inheritance."

2. We Must Go Back to the Old-Fashioned American Home to Grow Good Citizens

Lawlessness begins in the home. Child delinquency begins in the home. Children who are taught to respect, honor and obey the authority of the father and mother do not turn out as criminals.

Homes where children learn the Ten Commandments, learn the moral code of the Bible, learn to pray and sing gospel songs at a family altar do not produce drunkards, adulterers, profane swearers and infidels!

Where discipline is with firmness and love, where children are reared "in the nurture and admonition [or discipline] of the Lord," they learn that sin does not pay, that crime is punished, that nobody gets by with sin but must answer to God. You may be sure that no children reared by Susannah Wesley were criminals or divorcees or alcoholics or unbelievers.

And if I may be permitted a personal testimony, there is a logical and relevant reason why from my father's home there came out three sons for the ministry, one godly high school principal, another, a reverent deacon, and three noble women.

The same argument also applies to my own six daughters, all of them with fine records in college, all splendid musicians, all six married to ministers, three with books published, two with master's degrees.

Oh, the homes where stern, godly character is matched with family love, faithfulness, devotion to Christ and daily magnifying the Bible and prayer—such homes can turn the tide in America and help to stop the slide into perdition and ruin for our beloved country.

3. There Is a Solemn Duty in Christian Citizenship

It has been almost universally true in America that the greatest patriots were great Christians. Someone has said that the American Revolution was "a church revolution."

It is not wrong to be patriotic. Great men like Samuel Adams, John Adams, George Washington, Robert E. Lee, Stonewall Jackson, Abraham Lincoln, Woodrow Wilson, William Jennings Bryan loved America better because they loved God, believed the Bible and had solid Christian character.

I have no sympathy with the idea that America should give up her autonomy to be ruled by the United Nations or to make the law of United Nations supersede American law and American courts.

In the army I took a solemn oath to defend my country and to be true to it. The currents of my soul ran deep when I took that vow. I feel the same today. Oh, for a revitalized patriotism in America!

Every man should thrill to the flag, to the National Anthem, to the American Hymn.

HERE COMES THE FLAG!

Here comes the flag,
  Hail it!
Who dares to drag
  Or trail it?
Give it hurrahs—
Three for the stars,
Three for the bars.
  Uncover your head to it!
  The soldiers who tread to it
  Shout at the sight of it,
  The justice and right of it,
  The unsullied white of it,
  The blue and the red of it,
  And tyranny's dread of it!

Here comes the flag!
  Cheer it!
Valley and crag
  Shall hear it.
  Fathers shall bless it,
  Children caress it,
  All shall maintain it,
  No one shall stain it.
Cheers for the sailors that fought on the wave for it,
Cheers for the soldiers that always were brave for it,
Tears for the men that went down to the grave for it.
Here comes the flag!
                                    —Arthur Macy

I believe that the continually enlarged national debts in America are wrong and dangerous. I believe that the creeping socialism should alarm Christian people everywhere. I believe the encroachment of the central government on the rights of the states, and the effort of the President and the Supreme Court to control the schools, to change the laws by court interpretation, to dictate to state legislatures, ought to attract the attention and challenge the best efforts of Christian Americans to correct these dangers and evils.

The continual enlargement of our welfare rolls, the encouragement of people to be freeloaders, to believe that the government and the world owes them a living, are wrong. I believe good Christians should teach their children better than that and they should teach our politicians better, too.

Surely every Christian should remember the plain command to "submit yourselves to every ordinance of man for the Lord's sake: whether it be to the king, as supreme; Or unto governors, as unto them that are sent by him for the punishment of evildoers, and for the praise of them that do well" (I Pet. 2:13,14).

Every Christian ought to pray daily with supplications, prayers, intercessions and giving of thanks for all men and "for kings, and for all that are in authority; that we may lead a quiet and peaceable life in all godliness and honesty" (I Tim. 2:1,2).

I do not criticize our government's efforts to prevent the communists from getting a foothold in the Western Hemisphere. I do not criticize the earnest effort to stop the enslavement of Southeast Asia, in our defense of South Viet Nam. But I think that the safety of America will depend very largely on how Christian people pray day after day for the government of our land.

4. O Reader, Turn to the God of Our Fathers!

Let every Christian who reads this message be moved in heart to a new love for country, to a new sense of responsibility as a citizen of this country which God has so richly blessed. Yes indeed, "Blessed is the nation whose God is the Lord; and the people whom he hath chosen for his own inheritance" (Ps. 33:12). Let there be a personal renewal of our vows, a new dedication to God.

The better Christians we are, the better citizens we will be. The more we love God, the more we can help our children and neighbors and cities and towns and country to serve the Lord.

And all you who read this who have never personally trusted Jesus Christ, surely God wants you to repent today. Not only the nation but, even more, every unconverted individual should "prepare to meet [his] God." A study of the nations of the world proves again and again that God punishes sin but that "blessed is that nation whose God is the Lord" and that "righteousness exalteth a nation: but sin is a reproach to any people."

And if the nation is happy and blessed, which knows the Lord and serves Him, how much more is the eternal blessing of one who comes to know Jesus Christ as personal Saviour and who opens his heart's door to the Heavenly Guest!

We know that God loves our nation. He has blessed us with thousands of blessings beyond counting. But, poor lost sinner, God loves you personally. He sent His Son to die to save you: "For God so loved the world, that he gave his only begotten Son, that whosoever believeth in him should not perish, but have everlasting life" (John 3:16). I beg you to trust Jesus Christ to forgive you and then claim Him openly and set out to live for Him.

There is no use to grieve about the decline of the nation until you yourself turn to Christ, trust and love and serve Him. There is no making a godly America until we have godly individuals who have been washed in the blood and have taken Christ into their hearts by faith!

If you will here and now turn from your sin and trust the Saviour, I beg you, first, come to grips with the matter in your own heart and will. Do you now honestly choose to turn from sin? Do you here and now confess your poor lost condition, your need for a Saviour? And will you now, this moment, in your heart ask Jesus Christ to forgive you and save your soul? Then believe He does it because He said He would! "He that believeth on the Son hath everlasting life," He said in John 3:36.

HYMAN J. APPELMAN
1902-1983

ABOUT THE MAN:

Dr. Appelman was born in Russia and was reared and trained in the Jewish faith. He could speak many languages. The family moved to America in 1914. Dr. Appelman graduated with honors from Northwestern University and from DePaul University where he was one of the highest in the class and was awarded a scholarship. He received his license to practice law from DePaul Law School and was a trial lawyer in Chicago before his conversion—from 1921-25.

At age 28 he was converted. His Jewish family, then living in Chicago, disowned him. His father said to him, *"When your sides come together from hunger and you come crawling to my door, I will throw you a crust of bread as I would any other dog."*

Feeling a definite call to preach, he attended Southwestern Baptist Theological Seminary in Fort Worth from 1930-33.

In 1933 he was elected to be one of the State Evangelists for Texas; he faithfully ministered for eight years in this capacity for the Southern Baptist Convention. Later he launched into larger meetings, both in Texas and outside, and soon was spending some time, year after year, in a foreign country. His meetings were large meetings, with hundreds, sometimes thousands, of conversions in each.

Dr. Appelman made eight or nine trips around the world and several trips to Russia as an evangelist.

His schedule left one breathless. It was hard to find a day in his long ministry of fifty-three years that he was not preaching somewhere. He averaged two weeks at home out of a year. That was the intenseness of a Jew! Of this Jew, at least! His prayer life, hard work and biblical preaching reminded one of the Apostle Paul.

Dr. Appelman was the author of some 40 books.

VI.

Don't Sell America Short!

HYMAN APPELMAN

(Preached in the early 1970s)

"Blessed is the nation whose God is the Lord; and the people whom he hath chosen for his own inheritance."—Ps. 33:12.

America reminds one of the Jews in the time of David and Solomon. It has been most signally blessed of God. No other nation has grown to such titanic heights in so brief a time. It has never attacked first, never fought a war of aggression, never been the aggressor. No colonial area can accuse America of *"capitalistic disregarding of human rights and lives, of blood-sucking."* The Philippines, Cuba, Hawaii, Alaska—all are better off because of States' governmental control.

We have never lost a war, never sued for peace, never permanently given up an inch of territory, save by our own unconstrained will. Old Glory has yet to stoop before, to bow its proud colors to any conquering host.

England lost the great part of France it once owned. Frenchman William of Normandy conquered England, only to have his Franks swallowed, digested, made part of the rugged Anglo-Saxons. Spain, by papal decree, owned all of the new Columbus-discovered world save a tip of Brazil, where, to this day, Portuguese is spoken: but lost all of it.

America has grown from strength to strength. The stormy Atlantic on one side and the vast Pacific on the other, the tropical Caribbean to the south and the Canadian hugeness to the north, have watched the steady tread of Empire westward.

In a little over two hundred years of national existence, the government of every large nation has undergone a change—China, Japan,

Russia, Germany, France, England, Italy, Spain—but not America. Despite New Deals, packed courts, nepotism, crookedness in politics, in Union leaderships, grasping of capitalists and fifth columnists, the Declaration of Independence and the Constitution of the United States have stood fast as the Rock of Gibraltar. God was in the hearts of the men who followed John Hancock in taking their possessions, their liberties and their very lives in their hands, as they scrawled their bold signatures to the Declaration of Independence.

Face it! Recognize it! No country has ever produced so unselfish, so utterly devoted, so patriotic a leadership, at least not in as large numbers, as has this nation. Gentleman farmer George Washington, dubbed a traitor by his Britanic Majesty, leading the ragged Continentals to win a war, has not been excelled anywhere.

No one has ever equaled the miracle story of Abraham Lincoln, the commoner, the man of the very earth, the rivers, the lakes, the sun, the winds of the land that nurtured him, that honored him, that now bows at his feet, recognizing that once in many generations God brings to the forefront a man of such stature.

Americans are a separate breed, at times seemingly without a thought in their heads, bent on baseball, basketball, football, racing, then on the incarnadined battlefields of a world gone mad with the lust of war, writing a record of heroism, of utter abandonment of self, seldom, if ever, equaled in the annals of a war-wracked world.

Allow me to suggest this rather unique outline. First, What is America? Second, Where is America? Third, Why is America?

What Is America?

But, what is America? *It is a Dream!* It is the dream of a prisoner in his cell hoping, trusting, believing that someday one will come who will smash the door, break the shackles and relieve the galling bitterness of the endless days of bitter bondage.

It is the dream of the Christian suffering under the bigoted persecution of the narrow zealot who claims to be serving the lowly Nazarene by persecuting those with a differently crossed T, a differently sounded shibboleth, trusting for a land where he and his can serve God in spirit and in truth, in free growth of soul and spirit.

It is the dream of parents who, because of poverty, inequality, lack of opportunity, denied the privileges of higher education, are willing to make any sacrifices so that their children may not miss the chance of getting ahead, the chance at real living.

It is the dream of the patriot hating oppression with every drop of blood in his veins, willing to give his "last full measure of devotion" for the right to "liberty, equality and the pursuit of happiness," the unquestioned birthrights of all men, for so wrote old Tom Jefferson.

And these all together; multiply them by the oppressed of the earth; compare them to the sweep of tyranny, dictatorship, blood purges, megalomaniacs, Mussolinis, Hitlers, Lenins, Stalins and Khrushchevs, and you have the heart foundation of America.

Con the record of the heroes of all lands. Leonidas at Thermopylae; Horatius at the Tiber bridge; Alexander and his Phalanx; Caesar crossing the Rubicon; Harold Haddrada, the last of the Saxon kings; John Paul Jones and his *"We have not yet begun to fight"*; Lord Nelson, Lord High Admiral putting his spy glass to his blind eye to keep on fighting to victory, claiming he could not see the orders of the Admiralty. Great! Thrilling! Challenging! But these were trained soldiers. Compare them with the farm lads, the store clerks, the office men, the factory mechanics, their minimum of training, throwing back the Prussian military machine, Hitler's seemingly invincible armored divisions, step by bitter step, doggedly, bleedingly hedge-hopping the Pacific Islands, paying for every mile of return to the Philippines to echo the insistence of General Douglas MacArthur, *"We shall come back."*

You have to be born where I was (in Russia), under the despotic tyranny of a government that could not be any less concerned about the welfare, let alone the advancement, of its subjects, to understand fully the dream that is America.

America is an ideal. What our politicians are today, you judge; I am not prepared to debate on this. The Founding Fathers of our nation were, every one of them, idealists. Recall the replicas of the Declaration of Independence you have seen. Remember the signatures at the bottom, particularly the scrawled signature of John Hancock. This is the why of it.

The Declaration was a treasonable document. Whoever signed it immediately became a traitor against the British Empire, to have life, liberty, property, all, forfeited to the Crown, to be hunted down by the soldiers of the throned Hanovers.

The delegates in the Constitutional assembly in Philadelphia were not too eager to sign themselves traitors. After a protracted pause, John

Hancock, picking up the goose-quill pen, thrusting into the ink, exclaimed as he signed the Declaration, "We may as well hang together as hang apart." The others signed after him.

Those were idealists. George Washington, the second richest man in the Colonies, an officer in the British Army, took the commission of Commander-in-Chief of the Continentals, knowing that this would be considered the most traitorous act of all. Had he been caught, there would have been a worse fate for him than for Nathan Hale. Idealist that he was, super-patriotic in his devotion to the new land, he placed his name, his honor, his fame, his family, his fortune on the altar of patriotism.

America is an experiment. I come from a blood-stained continent that has never, in any generation, known complete peace. Its soil has been saturated with the blood, aye, fertilized with the bodies of the very best and choicest of its brave young, for that matter, old, too.

The Italians fight the Greeks. The Greeks fight the Turks. The French fight the Germans. The Russians fight the Poles and the Hungarians and the Finns. The English fight the Irish.

The same nationalities, with the same mores, the same blood, the same antecedents, the same traditions, come to the shores of these United States to form one nation "indivisible, with liberty and justice for all."

Sure, they fight each other, but not with guns, bombs, bayonets, bullets; but with ballots, with baseballs, footballs, basketballs, tennis balls. What is the difference? It can only be that the Almighty wants America— the Melting Pot of the nations—as an experiment in His hand for the rest of the world to learn the great lesson that men can and will live in peace and unity if they give God the chance. It is an experiment to see whether the common people, they of whom Abraham Lincoln said, "God must love the common people; He made so many of them," can be trusted with the ballot, with responsible governmental places, with authority, in civil and in military life.

It is an experiment in the hands of God, perhaps more aptly a blueprint, to show the world what He can do with a people who are willing to recognize His overlordship, His ownership, the devotion, the obeisance, the loyalty due Him. It is the opportunity for the Lord to pour out His blessings in riches, power and abundance such as no nation has ever known before.

Where Is America?

Today, in a storm-tossed world of conflicting ideologies, battling philosophies, where is America?

It is at the crossroads of the world's history. There was a time when men could rightly say, *"As goes England, so goes the world."* That is no longer true. England would be gone were it not for America, as would France and Germany and Italy and Spain. America is the deciding factor.

Russia is not moving its two hundred divisions, is not raining down its bombs because of America. China is not marching its six hundred million people to swallow, not only Tibet but India and Japan as well, because of America. There is no Jihad in the Near East, no Sadat, no al-Assad swallowing Israel. America will not permit it.

Don't sell America short! It is the deciding factor in and out of the Councils of the United Nations. America is at the crossroads to lead the world back into savagery or forward into sanity. Contrary to the harpings of the scientists who really ought to "stick to their lasts," it is not the cyclotron and the fearsome nuclear bombs that will decide the destiny of a world, but the attitudes, the ambitions, the activities of this colossus of the West.

America is at the end of four world wars: World War I and II, the Korean War and the Vietnam situation, where it has proved to the world a number of things. First, America is not imperialistic. It does not want anything others have. It does not want protectorates, colonies, the lands and the people of others. To be sure, on occasion, as now, American troops are policing a world. It is not because Americans actually want it that way. We should be more than glad to turn over this irksome responsibility to any other nation, to the United Nations, if either that nation or the United Nations could be trusted to maintain peace, to fend off aggression.

Four times our Big Brother Nation took up the cudgels for its weaker fellows, refusing to stand by, refusing to make merchandise, as it could have easily done, at the expense of the less fortunate. Four times, without thought of personal gain and at an unbelievably frightful cost in "blood, sweat and tears," in men and in money, America has shown the world it wants nothing but what is good for all. No one in his right mind, no one with the least sense of decency, with intellectual honesty, can possibly accuse America of imperialism. No people can say either to us or of us, "You took advantage of us. You attacked us. You played the bully."

Who stopped Wilhelm Hohenzollern and his spike-helmeted, heel-clicking, goose-stepping battalions astraddle bleeding Poland? AMERICA!

Who stopped Hitler, his Stukas, his Panzer divisions, his Dachaus, and Buchenwalds? AMERICA!

Who stopped Mussolini of the out-thrust Jaw and his 100,000 black shirts saluting the twentieth-century pseudo Caesar with their *"Moritur, te Salutamis,"* his rape of Ethiopia, his threat to dictate peace to the world at the tips of a million bayonets? AMERICA!

Who stopped Tojo—knave, black guard Tojo—and the puppet, polite-hissing, Myopie Mikado ordering the dastardly attack on Pearl Harbor? AMERICA!

But America has proven that it is not selfish, that it cannot carry a grudge. Let two men in Russia, the country of my birth, enter into a bitter fight with each other; let one knock the other one down, bloody him—they will be enemies for life. Let two simon-pure Americans engage in a fight; let one really overcome the other, prostrating him to the ground. When the fight is over, the winning American will help his erstwhile enemy to his feet, dust him off, to say, "Let's go have a cup of coffee."

The saddest mistake in American history came when the American troops were stopped at the Elbe River to give the Russians the chance to conquer their part of Germany. We could have, and we now realize we should have, conquered all of Germany. There would now be no West and East Germany, no West and East Berlin, no blood-splattered Wall, no fully-manned, fully-armed, fully-equipped communist divisions facing the skeleton United Nations (which, of course, means American) Division, with the threat of imminent conflict that might easily result in the Third World War.

Russia, on settling its tragic rule over East Germany, stripped it of its rolling stock of heavy agricultural and factory equipment, forcing numbers of Germany's highly trained scientists, industrial experts, superbly qualified mechanics, to sign papers declaring that they were crossing over behind the Iron Curtain of their own free will to work for the communist bosses, when any thinking person should know that they were forced to do so at the point of the bayonet.

America took over the West German sector. Before the barrels of the guns stopped glowing with the heat of the conflict, Americans were sending hundreds of millions in equipment and supplies to help West Germany rehabilitate itself.

The Japanese sneak-attacked us in the most dastardly violation of neutrality that history records. We lost scores of thousands of men, killed, maimed, missing in action, and billions of dollars. We drove Japan to its knees, forcing it to sign the peace treaty on the historic deck of the *Missouri*. Before the guns stopped belching their songs of death, the vast Pacific was plowed by American keels bringing what Japan needed to rebuild itself. Thank God for America! I am proud I can call myself an American.

America is climbing, still climbing in its standard of production and of living. America is not at the top of its prosperity. When the Democrats are in power, the Republicans sing the blues; when the Republicans are in power, the Democrats swing to the Cassandra song.

The commentators, newspapers, magazines, radios, televisions are all reflections, never completely honest, of the particular bias of their personal feelings. Do not take me wrong! With some, favorite reading is the sporting page, with others, the comics, with still others, the financial sections; with many, especially the ladies, the pages describing cooking, the home, fashions, social scandals. My favorite pages are those containing the editorials. Among other things, I want to know what to say, how to say it, how others are saying it, to influence opinion.

They tell us, well nigh unanimously, that America is facing bankruptcy. Reason this out if you please. A country that spends beyond thirteen billion dollars a year on alcoholic beverages is not about to go over the hill into the poorhouse. A nation that spends, in the face of cancer warnings, beyond seven billion dollars a year on tobacco, is not about to file for bankruptcy. A people that spends over six billion dollars yearly on cosmetics, much more than five billion dollars every year on dog food, a similar sum on dog medicines, is not about to stand on the street corners selling apples.

America is not at the height of its prosperity. Three generations from now, should the world stand that long, our great, great grandchildren will commiserate with us, as we are sorry for our great, great, great grandparents, as they marvel that we could live with what we had.

America is at the crossroads both politically and economically. It is further at the crossroads spiritually. There is not great fear in my mind that America will be taken over by communism or even by socialism.

When our President is seen to give away his personal wealth into either the socialistic or the communistic coffers, then shall I begin to become concerned over the takeover of our nation by either ideology.

When the Kennedy clan signs over its hundreds of millions to the groups named, then must we think long thoughts of the nation's becoming a prey to these foreign philosophies.

When the president of one great automobile concern signs over his $516,000 of one year's salary, and the president of another automobile manufacturing line his $293,000 annual salary to the treasuries of these un-American proposals, then is the time to become deeply concerned over the American way of life.

When the heads of the gigantic over-Labor Parties and others of their stature, men who turned down the United States State Department, absolutely refusing to confer with Khrushchev because he was "the head of a slave state," when these men assign their salaries of $90,000 annually, plus all sorts of fringe benefits, bringing their income to beyond $200,000 a year, to those in authority in either socialism or communism, then will I become alarmed over the prophecies of men who keep telling us that the Prussian's mad dream, voluminously set forth in *Das Kapital*, is upon us, but not until then.

What I am afraid of is paternalism, the philosophy that the world, to narrow it down, the nation, owes us a living, that we have the inalienable right to work little or not at all while the government cares for us from the cradle to the grave. More and more are subscribing to this shibboleth, failing or not caring to recognize that they are selling not only their birthright, but their very selves, for less than the proverbial mess of pottage, for so-called security that never fully materializes.

President Kennedy was right when he cried out, *"It is not ours to see, to demand, how much America can do for us, but on the other hand, to see how much we can do for America."*

Paternalism wrecked Rome with the games and the bread of the venial Caesars purchasing the votes of the fickle populace. God grant that America may think itself out of this dread hole of the pit in the cemetery of the nations.

America is at the crossroads spiritually. I maintain that America is not only the last bulwark on earth for democracy, it is also the last citadel for the propagation of the Gospel. Take one illustration.

In 1971, outside the Roman Catholic church, there were under 50,000 foreign missionaries in all the earth. Of these, by reputable report, more than 27,000 were from the United States. In addition to this fantastic preponderance of missionaries from this one nation, as compared with the rest of the world, America is raising more monies for missions, supporting more radio-world programs than all the rest of earth put together.

What would happen if the United States were not only to become confused with the terrible folly going the rounds of the death of God, but were to witness a regress in Christian fervor? What if the communists were actually to take over this country?

Why Is America?

Perhaps I should ask, "For Whom Is America?" History abundantly proves the contention that capitalism laid the foundation, built much of the superstructure of America's greatness—capitalism, with its generous investments in schools, in research in both the arts and sciences, with its plowing back into industry tremendous amounts of money, which then provide jobs, guarantees the nation's financial stability. You will argue with me that capitalism has not proved itself always an unqualified factor for good. I grant you that, even go beyond that.

There is something wrong with a capitalistic system when men, clowning to pamper perverted tastes, become millionaires; when women, prostituting the fair name of womanhood, marrying, divorcing, remarrying, with no more concern or consideration for that modesty which is the hallmark of decent womanhood, are featured, favored, feted, fortuned; when shaggy-haired quartets can become the rage of the day, sending not only teenagers but grown men and women into sexual hysterics. I shall be the first one to decry the antics of the age of capitalism when and where those animal-like actions are tolerated.

Then, if capitalism does not have the complete answer, suppose we try communism.

I am about communism as prize-fighter Joe Louis was about Hitler. Joe was a sergeant in the infantry during World War II. Someone asked him, "What do you think of Hitler, Joe?" After a bit of a pause, Joe drawled out, "There ain't nothing wrong with this country that that guy Hitler can straighten out."

There is nothing wrong with America that communism can straighten out. It has not yet succeeded in straightening out Russia, and for that matter, any other country it has taken over. We want neither hide nor hair nor shadow nor smell of the Kremlin crowd. They brag, compare, criticize—BUT COPY!

America is for capitalism, of course. Agreed are we all that capitalism has done a very great deal to raise our standards, to build our factories, our industries, our transportation. Capitalism has been the patron of schools, of libraries, of art institutes, of science. None of us deny that.

But is there not something wrong with a system that seems helpless in the face of entrenched crookedness, whose government, even in the highest places, is stopped by the flaunting authority of atheistic evolutionists, Tobacco Trust, Liquor Trust, Union bosses, by men in every leading sphere, men one step ahead of the police, the court, the prison cell?

Don't Sell America Short by Forsaking Our Christian Heritage

Is this the answer to the Tombs of the Unknown Soldiers before whose remains a nation keeps vigil day and night?

Is this what the ragged Continentals froze for, hungered for, bled for, lived and died for in the ice and snow of Valley Forge?

Is this what was in the minds of the men who responded to Abe Lincoln's call to save a nation with the song, "We are coming, Father Abraham, we are coming, one hundred thousand strong"?

Is this what seer and scholar Woodrow Wilson meant when he launched the best, the choicest, the finest manhood of America "to make the world safe for democracy"?

No! A thousand times no! Infinitely no! America is for Christ, our Lord and Saviour Jesus Christ. He is the only One worthy enough so that a free America can bow to Him without shame. He is the only One wise enough to lead us into the paths that will carry us to increasingly loftier heights—He is the only One able enough to command our men, our money, our very lives in whatever the future may hold for us.

The only way America can be sold short is by denying Christ His chance in the affairs of our land—and at this very day of national and international crisis. America cannot be, will not be sold short by any man or combination of men outside of its own shores.

God has not raised up this nation, blessed it beyond its fondest hopes, endowed it with a race of men and women such as have never peopled any other land—just to sell it short. Only Americans can help or hinder America. Only Americans can hurt our land. Only Americans can sell America short.

But, again, how? America is being sold short by crooked businessmen, by dishonest politicians, by schoolteachers, by college professors, who take advantage of immature minds to fill them with the poison of evolution, socialism, communism; by statesmen who compromise their principles—more and worse still—American principles; by so-called religious leaders who pollute the blessed Gospel of Jesus Christ with their vaporings of the Fatherhood of God and the brotherhood of man.

This all we know! But beyond that, America is being sold short by its millions of unsaved who, using our God-given prosperity, have launched a bacchanalia of sin that would shame Rome and Corinth and Babylon at their worst.

America is being sold short by the multitudes on the rolls of our churches who have never experienced the saving grace of Jesus Christ, who, bearing the holy name of the Son of God, belie their testimonies, befoul their professions, besmirch the fair name of their Saviour and Lord. These are in many ways worse than open sinners.

America is being sold short by Christians who are not "all out" for the Lord Jesus Christ, not loyal to their vows, not obedient to the commands of their Master, not true to the guidance of the Holy Spirit. They are soldiers "absent without leave," in their barracks, playing with things, while the thin ranks of their comrades strive to attack and are attacked on every front in their zeal for the kingdom of God and for the souls of men.

America must not be sold short. The soldiers of the cross true to their liege Lord must keep on regardless of consequences; striving, struggling, refusing to retreat, refusing to grow discouraged regardless of odds; refusing to do aught else but battle on. Then, it is for these, the true followers of Prince Immanuel, by their very zeal, by their very courage, by their conquering enthusiasm to enlist others under the oriflamme of the cross.

America shall not be sold short. So long as there is a Bible to cherish, a church in which to worship, a cross by which to be saved, a Holy Spirit to empower, a battle to fight, souls to save, a Master to follow, a Heaven to gain, hearts that love the Nazarene, that are concerned about the welfare of men, America must not be sold short.

The battle cry of our beloved nation should still be, at home and abroad, "If God be for us, who can be against us?" and, "Our God is a Man of War," and so He is, with all of the forces of the universe at His beck and call, with the resources of Heaven's treasuries at His command, with the legions upon untold, uncounted, because uncountable, legions of angels ready to obey His behest.

You have heard my plea. Will you agree with me then that it is no longer the religious duty but the patriotic duty as well of every American to pray for, to work for a national revival of religion that will insure our nation's, our people's being on God's side, that He in turn may be on our side? Will you enlist under the oriflamme of the cross of Christ, a Christian soldier, ready to join battle for God and for country?

Why I Love America

By a Russian Jew,
HYMAN APPELMAN

(Written in 1942)

Born in Russia, I came to the United States when I was twelve. I cannot tell you in detail why I love America, but every crimson drop of blood in my body carries that affection.

I LOVE AMERICA because of its greatness. It is great in territory, great in resources, great in man strength, great in woman beauty, great in child sweetness.

It is great in achievements, in accomplishments, in activities that have led the world in every line and sphere of human venture and adventure.

It is great in its history. Washington, Jefferson, Lincoln, Wilson—giants who stand out above the run of even the mighty!

America has never lost a war, never dipped its flag in any sort of defeat. From Bunker Hill to the Argonne, Old Glory has been covered with honor and praise.

I LOVE AMERICA because of its graciousness. America has shared its wealth, its scientific discoveries, its medical accomplishments, with all mankind. Pleas for help from many quarters of the world have been heeded.

Belgian children lived because American food ships landed on their shores.

German babies have grown into manhood (God forgive them for their ingratitude!) because with the signing of the Armistice in 1918 American relief lifted the hunger bans of that luckless land.

Starving Russians and emaciated Chinese knew hope when American soup kitchens lined them up for charity.

Japanese cities were rebuilt; Japanese homes were re-established;

Japanese men, women and children were given a new lease on life when the American Red Cross crossed the wide Pacific to bring help and hope.

I LOVE AMERICA because, at terrific sacrifice, it has been the world's Big Brother.

I LOVE AMERICA because of its gifts to me and to countless others. It gave me an education that I should never have had in Russia. It gave me a chance at freedom denied me as a Jew almost everywhere else in the world.

I LOVE AMERICA most of all because it gave me Christ and salvation. Here the Gospel was preached to me. Here the cross of the Lord Jesus was lifted up before me. Here salvation was proffered me as the gift of God's grace, backed up by yearning, loving anxiety of Christian hearts. Here waters of baptism laved me. Here that church welcomed me. Here the theological seminary opened its doors to me. Here I was and am, praise God forever, given the right to preach the burning conviction of my soul—that Jesus Christ, the Son of God, came into the world to save sinners.

You ask me why I love America?

The blood-marked sentry of George Washington's ragged Continentals hallowing Valley Forge is my answer.

The laconic report of Commodore Perry on Lake Erie, "We have met the enemy, and they are ours...," is my answer.

The Texans' cry, "Remember the Alamo," is my answer.

Abe Lincoln's "with malice toward none, with charity for all, with justice in the right as God gives us to see the right"—is my answer.

The bloody Meuse, Chateau Thierry, the Argonne, the Tomb of the Unknown Soldier, is my answer.

The handful of Marines on Wake Island holding back the yellow horde is my answer.

Douglas MacArthur and his sweat-stained, blood-soaked heroes in the foxholes of the Philippines is my answer.

You ask me why I love America?

I am a Jew! I am a Christian! Let the deep, fathomless depths of gratitude out of the very innermost being of my life, on my knees, on my face, thanking God for Christ, for the Constitution, for the Declaration of Independence, answer you, shout to you, rejoice with you—I LOVE AMERICA!

WILLIAM KENNETH MC COMAS
1929-

ABOUT THE MAN:

William Kenneth McComas was born just prior to the Great Depression. Denied a formal education largely due to poverty, he completed only eight grades of school in Wayne County, West Virginia. A physical breakdown at fourteen was followed by a disease diagnosed as incurable.

He felt, at an early age, that God had called him to preach, so he entered the ministry and became remarkably successful as a pastor, author and evangelist.

God has given this self-educated man an incredibly retentive and photographic memory. His sermons are spiced with colorful, illustrative language. And he writes the way he preaches.

Dr. McComas began the Calvary Baptist Church, Rittman, Ohio, in 1960 with eight members; today it boasts a membership of several thousand.

Before going into full-time evangelism in 1976, in addition to pastoring this large church, he conducted revival campaigns, preaching in many great churches. Also, he often spoke on college campuses and to civic organizations.

His prolific pen has produced many books. Somewhere on his agenda, he also found time to record twenty long-play stereo albums of his messages. Two of his patriotic sermons have been read into the *Congressional Record*. He holds an honorary Doctorate of Divinity and an LL.D. degree for outstanding achievements.

Dr. John Rawlings said of him: "I consider Dr. McComas one of the strongest men spiritually I have ever known. He lives and practices what he believes with a dedication to God that sets him apart from others."

VII.

Don't Hang the Black Crepe on America Yet...SHE IS NOT DEAD!

KENNY MC COMAS

"Blessed be the Lord my strength, which teacheth my hands to war, and my fingers to fight: My goodness, and my fortress; my high tower, and my deliverer; my shield, and he in whom I trust; who subdueth my people under me. Lord, what is man, that thou takest knowledge of him! or the son of man, that thou makest account of him! Man is like to vanity: his days are as a shadow that passeth away. Bow thy heavens, O Lord, and come down: touch the mountains, and they shall smoke. Cast forth lightning, and scatter them: shoot out thine arrows, and destroy them. Send thine hand from above; rid me, and deliver me out of great waters, from the hand of strange children; Whose mouth speaketh vanity, and their right hand is a right hand of falsehood. I will sing a new song unto thee, O God: upon a psaltery and an instrument of ten strings will I sing praises unto thee. It is he that giveth salvation unto kings: who delivereth David his servant from the hurtful sword. Rid me, and deliver me from the hand of strange children, whose mouth speaketh vanity, and their right hand is a right hand of falsehood: That our sons may be as plants grown up in their youth; that our daughters may be as corner stones, polished after the similitude of a palace: That our garners may be full, affording all manner of store: that our sheep may bring forth thousands and ten thousands in our streets: That our oxen may be strong to labour; that there be no breaking in, nor going out; that there be no complaining in our streets. Happy is that people, that is in such a case: yea, happy is that people, whose God is the Lord."—Psalm 144.

The United States of America was conceived in the hearts of God-fearing, freedom-loving men in lands across the sea. The labor pains were so severe that some thought she would be stillborn and succumb to terrible suffering. Baby America's proud fathers stood over her cradle and said, "We will name her *Republic* since she belongs to the people."

No sooner had the labor pains subsided and Baby America cried her first sounds of life, when a giant came stalking out of Europe with fire in his eyes and anger in his heart. That giant argued that America was not a Republic after all, but rather an apostate. He contended she had no right to live, and an immediate attempt was made upon her young life.

Miracle of miracles, that baby climbed out of her cradle, stated her position and slew the giant, as David did Goliath.

While she was still in her infancy, however, America was driven into the howling wilderness frontier. She struggled through disease, hunger, privation, poverty, bereavement and emerged with her spirits high.

From early childhood days, the going for America has never been easy. She has had wars from without and wars from within. She has suffered panics, depressions, droughts, earthquakes, devastating storms, dust bowls and floods. She has suffered earth-shaking political upheavals. She has had her "Boston Tea Party" and her teapot dome. She has had to deal with Benedict Arnold, Harry Dexter White, Alger Hiss, Julius and Ethel Rosenberg, Bobby Baker and John Erlichman.

Unfortunately, we still have to deal with John, Michael and Arthur Walker who jeopardized our national security and sold their birthright for a morsel of stew like Esau of old. Lonetree, Bracy and Stuffelbeam created the worst security breach in American Embassy history by laying their heads in the laps of Russian whores like Samson did Delilah. Thank God, they are the exception and not the rule. A bill has now been introduced in Congress to require the death penalty for anyone found guilty of espionage. America does learn from her mistakes.

America's critics have stood by with embalming fluid as skeptical religionists have assembled to offer the last rites and sing the requiem high mass.

Many doomsday prophets preached loud and long on America's self-destruction prior to her 200th birthday. They said she had aged so prematurely, she was tottering on her feet like a drunken man and would collapse right into the grave. Nineteen seventy-six came and went, however, and America still marches on.

As America celebrated her 204th birthday, she was experiencing her most degrading, devastating disaster. The world was stunned when a small band of radical militants, armed only with clubs and handguns, stormed the American Embassy in Tehran and took its occupants hostage. The Ayatollah Khomeini thumbed his nose at President Carter, the United Nations and the World Court. On April 25, 1980, America awakened to the sad news that a daring super secret, risk-laden rescue mission had ended in dreadful disaster. Perhaps the most shocking, saddest, sickening sight of all was when the Iranians publicly displayed the charred bodies of eight loyal American Marines in a spectacle of shame. Islam's god Allah was exalted and praised for his victory over the God of so-called Christian America.

While a pigmy held a prince hostage, the world seemed to say, "America has lost her clout and courage." Not so. On January 20, 1981, as Ronald Reagan was being inaugurated President of the United States, Khomeini reluctantly released our hostages. When the Commanding Officer of our rescue commandos was interviewed on public television, he said, "We had nearly a thousand more Marine volunteers than we needed for the mission. They understood quite well they may not come back."

When our Army liberated Granada, they displayed valor and won a great victory. When our Naval Air Force intercepted an Egyptian Boeing 737 in the dead of the night carrying a terrible terrorist with only fifteen minutes to accomplish their mission in international air space, they did it with perfect precision. Colonel Mummar Khadafy of Libya learned a little late we have big bombers with brave pilots as well as big naval guns fired by brave gunners. I don't necessarily agree with Napoleon that God is on the side of the biggest battalions, but I do contend that God has proven He is still on America's side.

America is not dead. We are one nation under God. America was God's gift to all people who love freedom. The broad stripes in Old Glory are sufficient to shelter everyone.

We have no room for little Russias, little Polands, little Italys, little Germanys nor little any other countries inside our boundaries.

Neither do we have room for those who come to our shores to eat our bounty and at the same time pull our house down upon our heads.

We have no room for those who will not uphold our principles of free government and want to enslave us to alien doctrines of dictators and tyrants.

We have no room for those who would stir up hatred and strife. I suggest they be given their tickets back to where they came from and sent there to stay. Too many believers today are emulating Elijah under the juniper tree. Their cry in self-pity is a long, loud and mournful "I ONLY REMAIN."

We need to take a second look at our great God, great land and great liberty. Most people who put up a strong argument against the Emory University professor by making a vibrant, verbal affirmation of faith in a living God, act as if they had just returned from His funeral. David said, "Blessed be the Lord my strength, which teacheth my hands to war, and my fingers to fight" (Ps. 144:1). That is a hot potato for the mealy-mouthed love doves from Congress, to the hippie camps that do not believe in defending our country. Is there any wonder David was probably the greatest soldier that ever marched? He had the best Instructor. "The Lord . . . teacheth my hands to war, and my fingers to fight."

American military leaders could say the same. God gave to our nation General Washington, General MacArthur and General Eisenhower—men who were on better speaking terms with God than they were with our Presidents. Our great military conquests have all been contingent upon the fact our generals could say with David, "Blessed be the Lord my strength, which teacheth my hands to war, and my fingers to fight."

Oh, yes, I know the argument of the skeptics quite well. They say America is not Christian anymore.

May I remind you, Mr. Skeptic, that America has more than 350,000 churches conducting services on a regular basis. She has an army of more than 373,000 ordained ministers. While it must be admitted they are not all fundamental, yet the largest Bible-believing, Bible-preaching churches in world history are in America today.

Young men and young women are surrendering to full-time Christian service in record number. America carries the mission load of the world. We provide the missionaries and money while we master every language under the sun to get the Gospel out. America does more Christian radio and television broadcasting than the rest of the world combined. We print and distribute more Bibles and Christian literature.

I submit to you, America is the greatest Christian nation in the world today. God has blessed, is now blessing and will continue to bless America. I am aware of the fact there is terrible sin in our camp. It can't go unnoticed that we have an escalated crime problem along with crooked politics and corrupted courts. But God has promised to bless America for her position. In Genesis 12:3, "I will bless them that bless thee, and curse him that curseth thee."

Ex-President Nixon must be given a great deal of credit for not surrendering to Arab blackmail tactics and bending to the pressures of our liberal Congress to desert the nation Israel. Please don't hang the black crepe on America so long as she tries officially to do right.

America's Hope Lies in Her Youth

David said, "That our sons may be as plants grown up in their youth" (Ps. 144:12). The Bible contains many special promises to young men. Joel said in his prophecy, "And it shall come to pass in the last days, saith God, I will pour out of my Spirit upon all flesh: and your sons and your daughters shall prophesy, and your young men shall see visions" (Acts 2:17; Joel 2:28). Solomon said, "Where there is no vision, the people perish" (Prov. 29:18).

God has given Christian young men in America a tremendous spiritual insight. God is not less intelligent than our military leaders. When there is a war to be fought, they call our young men whose vision is keen, legs are strong and hands are steady. They are not interested in older men whose lives have been spent. The Word of God makes an appeal: "My son, give me thine heart" (Prov. 23:26). The Apostle John said, "I write unto you, young men, because ye have overcome the wicked one" (I John 2:13). John goes on to explain his appeal to the young men: "...because ye are strong, and the word of God abideth in you" (I John 2:14). Paul wrote to Timothy, "Let no man despise thy youth; but be thou an example of the believers" (I Tim. 4:12).

Young men are more open-minded and receptive to challenge. Young men are not so sensitive because their ideas are preconceived. They are not self-made theologians who cannot be taught the Word of God.

A soldier from Indiana went down to West Virginia during the Civil War. Mortally wounded, he lay on a tree root for a pillow. A comrade gently placed his canteen to his lips. He pushed it aside and mumbled his mother's name and "Jesus." The cavalry at that instant marched by following "Old Glory" that was being whipped by the keen breeze. The dying soldier raised on his elbows and cried with great pathos, "Follow that flag, friend; I can die alone."

A chaplain was dressing the wounds of a soldier. The bridge of his nose had been shot off and both eyes blinded. Afraid to tell the wounded soldier, he whispered the sad news to his buddy. The wounded man overheard him and responded immediately, "If I had two more eyes, I would give them to keep my country free."

America still has an army of true-blooded young men, and you do not dare hang the black crepe on her door yet.

America's strength also lies in her

Godly Young Women

David said, ". . . that our daughters may be as corner stones, polished after the similitude of a palace" (Ps. 144:12). David was speaking of the beauty of young women. I am both happy and proud to say America still has beautiful young women. This is true in spite of Hollywood, women's lib and all the immodesty and immorality.

God wanted to give us a slight insight into Heaven's glory. To do so it was necessary to use a language of accommodation. In Revelation 21:2 John said, "And I John saw the holy city, new Jerusalem, coming down from God out of heaven, prepared as a bride adorned for her husband." The Song of Solomon depicts the beautiful relationship between Christ and His church by using the example of a beautiful woman and her lover.

The most beautiful thing God placed in this world is a pure, clean, beautiful and vivacious young lady. We live in a day when due respect is not always given. We need an Andrew Jackson to set the example of defense of his lovely Rachel, or even a Harry Truman who would fight for his Margaret. The first Adam gave up Paradise for a woman since he had not sinned, and he did it voluntarily. He could have refused the fruit, stayed in Paradise and been separated from his wife—but he chose to go with her. He said, "This is now bone of my bones, and flesh of my flesh. . . . Therefore shall a man leave his father and his mother, and shall cleave unto his wife" (Gen. 2:23,24).

This reminds us of the Second Adam who also gave up Paradise for a woman. In spite of the fact His lover, the church, was not all she should be, He loved her just the same. Young women in America play an important roll in our society. Thank God for good schoolteachers, Christian writers, nurses, lab technicians, secretaries; and we must recognize the fact that women carry much of the load in our Sunday schools today.

When William Booth was on trial in the Methodist Church for ministering to the ghettos, he had a choice to renounce his position or be excommunicated. His little wife Kathryn, in the balcony, cupped her hands over her mouth and yelled repeatedly, "Say NO, Will, say NO!" She helped him stand like a mighty fortress for God.

When Mrs. Ellet of Philadelphia was attending the funeral service of a grandson who had died in battle, she was asked by a reporter, "Are you bitter?" She momentarily became indignant, saying, "I have given two sons and four grandsons. If I had twenty, I would give them all to keep America free. If I were twenty years younger, I would gladly go and fight myself."

On that blessed morn of that early fall
When Lee marched over the mountain wall;
Over the mountains winding down
Horse and foot into Fredrick Town.

Forty flags with their silver stars;
Forty flags with their crimson bars
Flashed in the morning wind —
The sun of noon looked down and saw not one.

Up rose old Barbara Fritchie then,
Bowed with her fourscore years and ten,
Bravest of all in Fredrick Town
She took up the flag that the men hauled down.

In her attic window the staff she set
To show that one heart was loyal yet.
Up the street came the Rebel tread,
Stonewall Jackson riding ahead.

Under his slouched hat left and right
He glanced — the old flag met his sight.
Halt! The dust brown ranks stood fast.
Fire! Out blazed the rifle blasts.

It shivered the windowpane and sash;
It rent the panel with seam and gash.
Quick as it fell from the broken staff,
Dame Barbara snatched the silken scarf.

She leaned far out on the window sill
And shook it forth with a royal will.
"Shoot, if you must, this old gray head,
But spare your country's flag!" she said.

Don't hang the black crepe on America so long as she has this kind of women.

America's strength also lies in her

Bountiful Material Blessings

"That our garners may be full" (Ps. 144:13). Contrary to what most people are saying from the White House to the poorhouse, I believe America will be the last nation in the world to go hungry. Listen to the wise man Solomon: "The liberal soul shall be made fat: and he that watereth shall be watered also himself" (Prov. 11:25).

In spite of the fuel crisis in this country, we shared petroleum last year with other nations. Critics said we were foolish. God gave to us, however, the mildest winter in more than half a century. Every time America has given, God has vindicated the action.

I have enough Scotch blood in me to make me conservative religiously, politically and economically. I must confess, I joined the critics in lambasting Mr. Nixon for allowing Russia to have our excess wheat. Will you listen to our Lord: "Give to him that asketh thee, and from him that would borrow of thee turn not thou away" (Matt. 5:42)? Then will you listen to the wise man again: ". . . the borrower is servant to the lender" (Prov. 22:7). That makes every nation in the world a servant to the United States. Jesus said, "Give, and it shall be given unto you" (Luke 6:38).

No other nation has the agricultural technology of the United States. God has given us the know-how to produce 175 bushels of corn to an acre, 35 to 40 bushels of wheat to an acre and 40 to 50 bushels of beans to an acre. "The liberal soul shall be made fat."

It has been my privilege to travel through Europe, the Middle East, South America and many of the islands of the sea; and I have never seen a land with such obvious blessings of God upon it as the United States. Don't hang the black crepe on America so long as she is willing to share her blessings with others.

America's strength also lies in her

Christian Homes

The left-wing radical crowd pooled their ignorance and threw a scare into the American people, saying we would destroy ourselves by over-populating. That lie was obviously hatched in Hell. We have countless millions of acres of undeveloped land.

Christian mothers will continue having children, children who will be reared in Christian homes.

David said, ". . . that our sheep may bring forth thousands and ten thousands in our streets" (Ps. 144:13). That depicts godly mothers producing those precious little lambs. David also said, "Lo, children are an heritage of the Lord." When God wants a king, a military leader or a President, He can select a mother to produce him. Don't hang the black crepe on America as long as we have so many Christian homes.

In the last place, America's strength is in her

Willingness to Labor and Produce

"That our oxen may be strong to labour; that there be no breaking in, nor going out; that there be no complaining in our streets" (Ps. 144:14). The greatest war on poverty has been declared by America's work force. The major portion of our unemployment is from lack of desire to work. Paul said, 'If they don't work, don't let them eat.' We need some rigid laws to control our careless handouts and payment to people who loaf.

"That there be no breaking in. . . ." The Scripture here refers to our national defense. God has given us the technical know-how to produce hydrogen missiles, planes and atomic submarines. He expects us to use them wisely in our national defense. He expects those men yonder at the North Pole to be alert twenty-four hours a day as they operate our DEW line defense program.

Our hope, however, is not in these manmade destructive and protective instruments. David said, "The Lord. . .my fortress; my high tower, and my deliverer; my shield, and he in whom I trust" (Ps. 144:1,2).

When our Pilgrim Fathers were nearing the coast of Massachusetts, they knelt in the Mayflower for prayer, then drafted a sacred document which began with these words, "In the name of God, Amen." That gave America a solid foundation. David also said, ". . .that there be no complaining in our streets."

The most damaging, destructive thing that can happen to America is for our citizens to run around magnifying our weaknesses and faults. Our enemies can do that quite well. They really don't need any help from the inside. The Word of God clearly commands that we uphold our national leaders in prayer, yet untold thousands who call themselves fundamental Christians criticized Mr. Nixon without once going to God in prayer in his behalf. If our leaders fail, it is because the church has failed. President Ford testified to the whole nation that his schedule never becomes too busy for him to take time out to go to prayer meeting on Wednesday night. I dare say, many of our Baptist people cannot say the same, and yet they will criticize him.

Man's only unsinkable hope is in God. On April 10, 1912, 2,200 tourists boarded a ship at South Hampton, England. There was a collective wealth among those men which exceeded 20 million dollars. That ship was a floating palace with ankle-deep carpet. It had all the facilities of a small town. It was referred to as a floating Babylon. She was 882 feet from the bow to stern, weighing nearly 47,000 tons, and was 11 stories high. One crewman said, "Even God couldn't sink this ship."

On the fifth night of her voyage, however, the Titanic crossed paths with a huge iceberg in the cold North Atlantic waters. A 300-foot gash was cut in her side. The band which had been playing happy ragtime music soon changed to "Nearer My God to Thee."

The "Ship of State" has been hit by a terrible iceberg. The waters are running in, but if God was willing to spare Sodom for ten righteous people, surely He will spare America.

Don't hang the black crepe yet.

(You may have the above message in booklet form for $1.00, or on cassette for $5.00. Order direct from Dr. Kenny McComas, 500 West Sunset Drive, Rittman, OH 44270.)

VIII.

"Put None But Americans on Guard Tonight"

KENNY MC COMAS

"And Moses was learned in all the wisdom of the Egyptians, and was mighty in words and in deeds. And when he was full forty years old, it came into his heart to visit his brethren the children of Israel. And seeing one of them suffer wrong, he defended him, and avenged him that was oppressed, and smote the Egyptian: For he supposed his brethren would have understood how that God by his hand would deliver them: but they understood not."—Acts 7:22-25.

America's Founding Fathers supposed that our citizens in 1987 would understand that they had laid their very lives on the line to guarantee our freedom, but we understand not. We failed to heed the admonition of General George Washington when he said, "Put none but Americans on guard tonight." We have stationed chicken thieves at the henhouse door to guard our chickens. When Senate Majority Leader Robert Byrd of West Virginia voted to give our Panama Canal away, he was asked by newslady Barbara Walters if it did not concern him that 73 percent of his constituents opposed the canal give-away. His prompt reply was, "I could care less how the people in West Virginia feel. I vote the way I want."

Whatever happened to the voice of "We the people of the United States"?

For the advancement and security of our people, the great Teddy Roosevelt, who walked softly but carried a big stick, oversaw the construction of the canal. As a nation, America paid dearly for that waterway. We first purchased and paid for the construction site from the Panamanian government. When their citizens complained that the property was not their government's to sell, we purchased and paid for it again.

Working conditions were at their worst. Malaria-carrying mosquitoes were swarming uncontrollably. Some engineers and overseers could only come to land once every six months. Many workers died in those humid, highly infectious conditions. We are still paying on the bond debt for construction, yet President Jimmy Carter was audacious enough to tell the American people we never owned the canal.

We need to put only Americans on guard tonight.

Religion played a vital role in the lives of the framers of the Constitution. Only one of the 39 signers was not affiliated with a major denomination. They chose to articulate the date of that sacred document in this manner, "Done in convention by the unanimous consent of the states present the Seventh Day of September in the YEAR OF OUR LORD. . . ." Of the various churches to which the signers belonged, all had two important doctrines in common: (1) the existence of a triune God; (2) the deity of Jesus Christ the Lord.

Just being born or naturalized an American citizen does not qualify one for guard duty. Jonathan Pollard was American-born, but in 1985 he was arrested and later convicted for selling top military secrets to Israel. For a meager $50,000, he was willing to jeopardize the security of every freedom-loving American.

On December 15, 1791, ten amendments were made to the Constitution. The first reads as follows, "Congress shall make no law respecting an establishment of religion, or prohibiting the free exercise thereof." Because we allowed atheists and others of foreign persuasion to guard our religious freedoms, we have over 4,700 court cases pending against our citizens who exercised their constitutional religious rights.

On January 29, 1919, after a careful analysis of what alcohol was doing to our great nation, our legislators ratified the Eighteenth Amendment to the Constitution. The sale or transportation of all intoxicating liquors was strictly forbidden within the boundaries of the continental United States. They knew a drunken nation will eventually fall into the ditch of destruction to lie in its own vomit.

Then came Franklin D. Roosevelt with his wheeling and dealing team of "new dealers." Mr. Roosevelt went on American radio and pathetically appealed to the nation to go to the polls and repeal the 18th Amendment. He promised the people that alcohol would never again be sold by the drink. He convinced the rank and file we needed alcohol revenue to stimulate a sick economy. Shortly after the repeal, on December 5, 1933, 270,000 saloons were selling alcohol by the drink.

Today, we carry a back-breaking tax burden trying to build hospitals, clinics and treatment centers for our more than 25 million alcoholics. The unknown poet left these lines behind in "THE DRINKING HOUSE OVER THE WAY":

> **He wants to do right, but you never could think**
> **How weak a man grows when he's fond of the drink.**
> **It's tempting him here and it's tempting him there—**
> **Four places I've counted on this very square—**
> **Where a man can get drink by night or by day,**
> **Not to mention the drinking house over the way.**
>
> **I fell on my knees, I cried and I prayed,**
> **While he in a smoke-filled room by his booze bottle stayed.**
> **My room was so lonely, so quiet and still,**
> **As my thoughts went back to my home on the hill.**
> **The men who made laws, sir, sure didn't think**
> **Of the hearts they would break and souls they would slay,**
> **When they licensed that drinking house over the way.**

Let's put only Americans on guard tonight.

A very subtle, highly organized plan is now under way to abolish the old and rewrite a new Constitution. About 30 persons of powerful political persuasion met on December 5, 1986, at the Mayflower Hotel in Washington, D. C. The meeting and its purpose was not made public until January 11, 1987, when *The New York Times* gave it front-page coverage. One of the meeting members is quoted as saying, "We are the parliamentary government group."

They openly assert that our Constitution impedes solutions to many of today's problems and needs drastic changes. This group obviously sees itself as having the foresight of James Madison, Alexander Hamilton, Benjamin Franklin and other Founding Fathers who met at the Constitutional Convention in Philadelphia 200 years ago. The official title of the group is *COMMITTEE ON CONSTITUTIONAL SYSTEM.*

Lloyd N. Cutler is identified by *The New York Times* only as "a prominent Washington attorney," but he happens to be the Chairman and driving force behind the group. Other key figures include Former Secretary of the Treasury C. Douglas Dillon; Former World Bank President Robert S. McNamara; leading liberal Senate internationalist for many years, J. William Fulbright; Senators Daniel Patrick Moynihan of New York and Charles Mathias, Jr., of Maryland; former leading internationalist in the House of Representatives for many years, Henry Reuss; former Pennsylvania Governor Dick Thornburgh; and James MacGregor Burns, a historian who is often quoted by *The New York Times*.

The CCS has been kicking around their radical ideas for at least ten years, but now they are down to serious business.

In 1985, the Committee on Constitutional System published a book entitled, *Reforming American Government*. They make no bones about their dissatisfaction with our present Constitution. In discussing the Constitution they use such terms as "problems," "crises," "reform," "defects," "decay," and "risk," only to mention a few. It is quite clear they think our present Constitution is outmoded and inadequate. We must, therefore, by all means put none but Americans on guard tonight.

It was in the very early hours of the morning when the American news media first learned that two Russian cosmonauts had gone into space. A reporter called our space control tower in Houston for their reaction. The officer yawned and said, "No comment. We've been sleeping."

Sleep is an act of the most natural kind, but we dare not sleep when our enemies are on the prowl. The Old Book that's always up-to-date has a stout, stunning, soul-stirring word of warning to America in 1987. The Prophet Isaiah sounds as if he is writing the cover story on our American Embassy in Moscow:

"His watchmen are blind: they are all ignorant, they are all dumb dogs, they cannot bark; sleeping, lying down, loving to slumber. Yea, they are greedy dogs which can never have enough, and they are shepherds that cannot understand: they all look to their own way, every one for his gain, from his quarter. Come ye, say they, I will fetch wine, and we will fill ourselves with strong drink; and to morrow shall be as this day, and much more abundant."—Isa. 56:10-12.

Samson had all the makings to become Israel's greatest judge, but sleeping on the lap of a whore while his enemies plotted against him destroyed all his potentiality. Righteous Lot vexed his soul while sleeping in Sodom, and when he finally awakened and attempted to sound an alarm, no one would listen.

The persons of the pulpit in America have been sleeping for the most part. We either have no comment or we can't get anyone to listen. Those messenger slaves we know as ether waves have been burdened recently with scandal. Someone facetiously said, "We've had Watergate, Irangate and now Pearly Gate."

Put none but Americans on guard tonight.

Reframers of our Constitution didn't appear only yesterday. The Ford Foundation financed extensive studies at the Democratic Institutions in Santa Barbara, California, throughout the '70s, which produced 40 separate drafts of a new Constitution. The original project was headed by Rexford Guy Tugwell, a prominent member of Franklin D. Roosevelt's "Brain Trust" during the '30s.

The liberal internationalists made a serious attempt to use the bicentennial of the Declaration of Independence in 1976 to their advantage in rewriting the Constitution. The World Affairs Council of Philadelphia published a "Declaration of INTERdependence" and persuaded 104 Congressmen and senators to sign it. The signers included such famous names as Alan Cranston, Hubert Humphrey, George McGovern, Walter Mondale, John B. Anderson, Les Aspin and John Brademas.

The book published by The Committee on Constitutional System, entitled, *Reforming American Government*, features Robert S. McNamara on the book cover. It should be noted that McNamara was head of Ford Motor Company during the Edsel years of embarrassing failure. He was Secretary of Defense from 1961 to 1967 under Presidents John F. Kennedy and Lyndon Johnson. Those are the years Russia gained an eight-to-one military advantage over the United States. McNamara then became President of the World Bank, where he played Santa Claus by giving our money to anyone who held up a stocking.

Just listen to what this Constitutional authority had to say about our Constitution: "It is tempting to believe that our Constitutional System, having survived for almost 200 years, can handle the daunting challenges it now confronts. But common sense warns us that it may not be so." Just a subtle way of saying our Constitution is not adequate to handle today's challenges.

Put none but Americans on guard tonight.

When we express concern, they say we have nothing to worry about, just go on back to sleep.

But they have the same stripe as the crowd who said, prior to World War II, "The Maginot line is quite impregnable, and Hitler's forces could never touch France"; but they did.

They said General Mudd would easily defeat the Nazi invaders of Poland, but he did not.

They said tanks could never cross the Dutch Canal or the Greek mountains, but they did.

They said no military power could ever take Singapore, but they did.

They said the Philippines could easily be defended, but they were not.

They said airplanes could never sink a battleship, but they did.

They said Germany would run short of petroleum before the end of 1940 and all her aggression would suddenly cease, but it did not.

They said we should not fret about the little island of Japan—that she could be easily defeated in three weeks to six months. In reality, it took 3½ years of mingling the blood of American boys with the mud of the South Pacific.

They said the Dutch West Indies would fight off all enemy attacks, but she did not.

Dr. Albert Heimer, Professor of History at the University of Michigan, said, "The United States for many years has been dominated to a large extent by persons who do not understand the spiritual heritage bequeathed by their own ancestors. Unless a marked change takes place soon, the United States is doomed as surely as ancient Babylon." That doesn't happen to be the words of a loud-mouth fundamentalist.

Put nothing but Americans on guard tonight.

Dr. Luke the human author, under the inspiration of the Holy Spirit, said, "For he [Moses] supposed his brethren would have understood . . ." (Acts 7:25). Don't expect others to understand when you defend the Constitution and exercise your rights provided for in it.

The Committee on the Constitutional System is standing by like vultures waiting to converge on a carcass. Our United States is now perilously and fearfully on the brink of being swept into another Article V Amendment, which requires the calling of a Constitutional Convention. Thirty-two state legislatures have already passed resolutions calling for a Constitutional Convention for the purpose of balancing the budget. If two more states pass a similar resolution, Article V requires Congress to call a Constitutional Convention. If it happens, our Constitution will be up for grabs.

The Committee on the Constitutional System has a lot of tall players on their team. Their game strategy is to look like kittens but play like tigers. Grantland Rice, the renowned sports writer of the past, said, "When the great Scorekeeper comes to write against your name, it matters not if you won or lost, but how you played the game."

It matters a great deal in this case as to whether we win or lose; therefore, put none but Americans on guard tonight.

A. LOYD COLLINS
Died in 1979

ABOUT THE MAN:

This inspiring lecture, "The Hand of Almighty God in American History," was widely given in many parts of the United States in churches, at religious conferences, and in schools and colleges.

It is by a well-known author, lecturer, minister, historian and educator—Dr. A. Loyd Collins who was Dean of the School of Arts and Sciences at Springfield Baptist College, Springfield, Missouri. It is based upon his book, *God in American History*.

Dr. Collins lectured throughout the United States and in many foreign countries, including Canada, Old Mexico, Scotland, England, Holland, Belgium, Germany, Liechtenstein, Luxembourg, Austria, Switzerland, Italy, and France.

He held the A.A., B.S., M.A., LL.B., Ph.D. and Th.D. degrees and many honorary degrees, including LL.D., D.D., Litt.D., HH.D., etc.

This dedicated Christian was a great preacher, soul winner and orator.

IX.

The Hand of Almighty God in American History

A. LOYD COLLINS

When freedom from her mountain height
Unfurled her standard to the air,
She tore the azure robe of night,
And set the stars of glory there.
Breathes there the man with soul so dead
Who never to himself hath said,
"This is my own, my native land"?

"Blessed is the nation whose God is the Lord; and the people whom he hath chosen for his own inheritance."—Ps. 33:12.

The United States of America is a great and a glorious nation. God has made it magnificent. We proudly sing, "My country 'tis of Thee, sweet land of liberty," and with patriotic pride we behold the beautiful Stars and Stripes as they in triumph wave with resplendent glory "o'er the land of the free and the home of the brave."

I firmly believe that the Almighty has made America His chosen land. There has been none other like it in all of the annals of the history of human civilization. It has been showered with an abundance of blessings far beyond the power of the comprehension of man.

The Lord has made America great. He has truly made it a land of honey—with sheep upon a thousand hills—with waving field of golden grain—with the boundless prairies of the West—with the timber giants of the North—and the white cotton fields of sunny Dixie: a land of peace and of love and song where we live like kings and queens.

What is the secret of our national success and greatness? It is to be found in our trust and faith in God. There is no substitute for the religion of Almighty God; it is the Alpha and the Omega, the beginning and the end.

From the days when the bold and courageous Christopher Columbus sailed the unchartered waters of the stormy Atlantic until the present hour, we have looked above for the guidance of our life and destiny
as a people and later as a glorious Republic founded upon the principles of democracy, justice, faith and freedom.

Columbus believed in God and trusted in Him on his great voyage
across the unmapped waters of a great, foaming, unknown ocean. The
log of Columbus for Wednesday, October 10, 1492, two days before
his historic discovery, reveals that he "was going to continue until he"
reached his goal "with God's help."

The first thing that they did when they reached the shores of America
was to fall down upon their knees in the sands by the seashore and
thank God for His guidance and help.

The same deep religious spirit promulgated our early settlers. The
first charter of Virginia, dated April 10, 1606, indicates that one of the
purposes of English Colonization in America was for the propagation
"to Christian religion" for those who lived "in darkness and miserable
ignorance of the true knowledge and worship of God."

When Mrs. Collins and I visited beautiful and picturesque Jamestown
Island in Virginia, the place of the first permanent English settlement
in this country, one of the first and most impressive things that we saw
was the old vine-covered Jamestown Church and the memorial tablet
which depicts the scene and spot on the island where the first commu-
nion service was held June 21, 1607.

The story of another English colony is even more dramatically
known—that of the Pilgrim Fathers at Plymouth, Massachusetts. When
the courageous men and women landed here amid the ice, the sleet
and the snow, they got down on their knees and asked God to direct,
to support and to help them. No wonder the poet has said:

> **Aye, call it holy ground,**
> **The spot where first they trod,**
> **For there they left unstained**
> **What there they found—**
> **Freedom to worship God.**

Even before they landed at Plymouth Rock, they met in the cabin
of their historic little ship and there drew up one of the greatest
documents in all American history, known as the "Mayflower Compact"
(1620). They said that we have undertaken this little settlement of ours
on wild and virgin shores of a strange land . . . "for the glory of God

and the advancement of the Christian faith."

It is a matter of historical record that in nearly all of the early charters and grants of land in America, a missionary purpose was expressly pointed out; that was one of the primary objectives of colonization.

Their noble work did not go without reward. It was an Indian, converted to the Christian faith, who prevented the complete annihilation of the Colony of Virginia in 1622 by warning the settlers of a pending Indian attack.

No institution has really contributed more to the genuine resplendent grandeur of America than has the church of Almighty God.

Famous churches have written a glorious chapter in American history. It has been my privilege to have visited many of these churches. In Boston, we saw the Old South Meeting House, where Samuel Adams and others spoke out against injustice and British oppression; we have also been at the Old North Church, and I climbed up into the steeple where the signal lanterns were hung to warn the patriots of the coming of the British. In Philadelphia, we were in Christ's Church and sat in the pew where Washington worshiped. In Richmond, we stood by the seat where Patrick Henry shouted: "Give me liberty, or give me death!"

All throughout our colonial days, the church was paramount, and religious worship was an integral part of the daily life of the people. They clung to their faith, looked above and courageously forged ahead, undaunted and unafraid. As soon as homes were erected, meeting houses were built in which to worship God who, with His divine hand, had led them all along the way. The Holy Bible was a "light unto their path" and the eternal Guide Book for their lives. No wonder the songwriter wrote, "How Great Thou Art!"

The trials, vicissitudes and problems were many; but they put their trust in the Lord, and He saw them through. He upheld and sustained them with His omnipotent hand.

When troubles with the mother country, England, mounted and were intensified and when at last the colonists met for the First Continental Congress in Carpenter's Hall in Philadelphia, 1774, the chaplain got down on his knees in the center of that little hall, and all of the members of Congress got down on their knees around him and asked for the help of Almighty God in their undertakings.

Many times, when I have stood in that Hall, I have thought of how God heard the prayers of those noble old patriots of the long ago.

As the "last stars were vanishing from night" before the Battle of Lexington and the messengers ran to the village green with news of the approaching British, the old sexton ran to the church and rang the bell in the steeple, calling the patriots to form in battle line; their minister was there with them carrying his old flintlock musket.

The evening before the Battle of Bunker Hill when the twilight came and the Army gathered upon Cambridge Common before proceeding to fortify the hill, they paused, took off their hats and were led in earnest prayer by Chaplain Langdon, President of Harvard College.

After Washington had crossed the ice-filled Delaware in 1776 and won the great victory at Trenton, he raised his eyes to Heaven, it is said, and thanked God for the victory.

In front of Independence Hall, I purchased from a man, whose hair has been whitened by the snows of many winters, a reproduction of the original copy of the Declaration of Independence. The parchment upon which the first copy was written has yellowed with age, and the signatures of many of its illustrious signers have almost faded away, but its principles live today, as never before, in the history of the world. I carefully read that precious document through once again. At the end are these words: "For the support of this declaration" we look "with a firm reliance on the Protection of Divine Providence."

During the darkest days of the American Revolution at Valley Forge, the lone sentries slowly walked back and forth in the dim star-lit night leaving stains of blood where their bare feet passed over the cold snow-covered ground.

One day a farmer came home and said to his wife, "Mother, the British are going to lose this war."

"What makes you think so, John?" was her reply.

"Because," said he, "I saw George Washington today down on his knees in the snow praying to God for guidance and help. A faith like that cannot be defeated."

We have depended upon the Lord, and He has always helped us as a nation. Our great leaders have had faith in and have trusted Almighty God to lead and to direct them. As the old Ship of State has been guided through troubled and foaming waters of storm and strife, it has looked above, and it has sought the hand of the Almighty to steady the wheel.

Abraham Lincoln said one time: "I do not know where the Ship of Life will finally take me; but there is one thing that I do know: I know the Pilot of that ship, and I have been assured all along the way by the touch of His hand on mine."

President William McKinley, upon his deathbed, is reputed to have said: "It is God's way, and I today am clinging to my Father's hand, for I know the way I go leads to that better land." What a blessed assurance!

Before Pickett's historic charge of Gettysburg, the Confederate chaplain advanced to the long lines of gray and got the men down on their knees and led them in prayer. A few minutes later one of the field commanders rode along the lines. A captain said to him, "General, this is a desperate charge."

"True," said he, "but the issue is with the Almighty, and we must leave it in His hands."

That is true of many of our grave problems today.

A foreigner once came to our shores because he wanted to try to discover the real secret of the greatness of America. After visiting with many of our leaders and traveling through many sections of our country, he said that he had discovered the real secret of the greatness of America—our faith in God.

Franklin D. Roosevelt said that the Bible was our "fountain of strength."

I was a close personal friend of former President Harry S. Truman. Shortly after he became President, he told me: "I want you to pray that God will always give me the wisdom to make the right decisions for the welfare of our country."

The Bible was always on his desk in the White House, and he read from it daily.

Before President Dwight D. Eisenhower gave his inaugural address, you will doubtless recall that he first paused and offered a prayer for God's help and leadership.

In the trying days of the Civil War, a man once said to President Lincoln: "I'm glad that God is on our side."

But Mr. Lincoln's reply was: "What I'm concerned about, brother, is that we are always on God's side."

These are trying times in which we live. War clouds hang darkly overhead. What is the answer to our grave problems? Is there any way out?

Hear the ringing words of that great apostle of peace, Woodrow Wilson. The words that he wrote nearly a half a century ago are as true today as they were in 1923.

Our civilization cannot survive materially unless it is redeemed spiritually. It can be saved only by becoming permeated with the Spirit of Christ and being made free and happy by the practices which spring out of that spirit. Only thus can discontent be driven out and all the shadows lifted from the road ahead.

It is our challenge to keep America spiritually great.

While in the service, a boy said to me: "You don't have anything to cling to unless you have God."

I read a letter a soldier wrote to his mother. It said: "Don't merely pray that I will come back, Mother. I want you to pray that I will have the courage to do my duty whenever the time comes."

It was boys with Christian fathers and mothers like that who carved this country of ours out of the wilderness. They plowed the virgin lands with ox teams and made the prairie blossom like the rose. They built our great cities, established our industries and eventually pushed civilization across the waters of the majestic Mississippi to the white-capped waves of the Golden Gate on the Pacific. They fought for the great heritage which is ours today.

I hear the sharp report of their muskets along the lanes of Lexington as they poured out their life's blood on the village green. They stood at Concord Bridge, immortalized by the thrilling, dramatic lines of Ralph Waldo Emerson:

By the rude bridge that arched the flood,
Their flag to April's breeze unfurled,
Here once the embattled farmers stood
And fired the shot heard 'round the world.

They bled on the slopes of Bunker Hill that hot day in June, 1775. They shivered around the campfires amid the sleet and snows at Valley Forge. They held the broken line at Shiloh and climbed the flame-swept hill at Chattanooga. They planted the Stars and Stripes on foreign fields amid the crimson flare in 1917. They died on the shores of Battan and opened the beachhead at Normandy.

The names of most of them today are to be found in the garden of memories inscribed upon tablets of stone, amid the flowers that love has planted and love has plucked "on fame's eternal camping ground"; but their spirit lives on as a challenge to us.

Such has been our struggles and heritage with the help of Almighty God.

In the darkest hours of the conflict in World War II, MacArthur, in reporting his military victories, always said: "By the help of God," we have been able to do thus and so.

The poet has said:

> **Right forever on the scaffold,**
> **Wrong forever on the throne,**
> **But the scaffold holds the future,**
> **And behind the dim unknown**
> **Standeth God within the shadows**
> **Keeping watch above His own.**

The lessons of centuries of history stare us in the face. The pyramids of ancient Egypt stand as tombstones to a great civilization that was and is no more.

The splendor of Babylon and Assyria has passed away.

The great Chinese Wall has crumbled into dust.

Greece, at one time the most intellectual nation in the entire world, is today but a fading and miserable shadow of her former greatness.

Mighty Rome, extending from north to south, from east to west— what do we find of it today? Nothing but crumbled ruins where once the scepter of the Caesars swayed the destiny of the world.

You ask, "Will the same be true of America? Will students of history living in future generations read and study about the rise and fall of the United States?"

I can give you a clear-cut answer: As long as we stay close to God, our nation will live and prosper and thrive. The history of America has exemplified that "righteousness exalteth a nation."

If we continue to look into the face of God and follow His teachings, He will bless us; He will make us great and a blessing to all mankind.

When at last it becomes twilight upon the trail of the twentieth century and the evening shadows slowly gather and we hear the fading echo of bygone bugles and the beat of muffled drums telling of the death of an old century; and when in splendor and greatness the twenty-first century is born, I believe that Old Glory will still be waving in the sky. I believe the Christian flag will still be waving there. But it is up to us, in our own small way, to help to keep them waving there.

This is an age of new isms, new theories and strange philosophies of government. The challenge is to all mankind.

I decline to help set up in this country any government greater than that established by our Forefathers of the long ago, baptized in fire and blood from the village green of Lexington to the jungles of Viet Nam and sanctified by the tears of American mothers whose sons have gone down beneath the Stars and Stripes to sustain its honor and its glory—the government of the United States of America.

America, America, we claim thee as our own.
For thee we face the cannon's mouth and scorn the monarch's throne;
But lest like bygone nations thou dost lose thy proud estate,
We humbly ask for guidance from the God who made thee great.

Duty — Honor — Country

DOUGLAS MacARTHUR

(On May 12, 1962, he was awarded the Sylvanus Thayer Medal, the highest honor of the United States Military Academy. That day, the General reviewed the Corps of Cadets on the Plain at West Point, lunched with them at the mess hall, and then responded to the presentation with these remarks:)

Duty—Honor—Country. Those three hallowed words reverently dictate what you ought to be, what you can be, what you will be. They are your rallying points to build courage when courage seems to fail, to regain faith when there seems to be little cause for faith, to create hope when hope becomes forlorn. Unhappily, I possess neither that eloquence of diction, that poetry of imagination, nor that brilliance of metaphor to tell you all that they mean.

The unbelievers will say they are but words, but a slogan, but a flamboyant phrase. Every pedant, every demagogue, every cynic, every hypocrite, every troublemaker and, I am sorry to say, some others of an entirely different character, will try to downgrade them even to the extent of mockery and ridicule.

But these are some of the things they do. They build your basic character; they mold you for your future roles as custodians of the nation's defense; they make you strong enough to know when you are weak and brave enough to face yourself when you are afraid.

They teach you to be proud and unbending in honest failure, but humble and gentle in success, not to substitute words for actions, not to seek the path of comfort, but to face the stress and spur of difficulty and challenge; to learn to stand up in the storm but to have compassion on those who fail; to master yourself before you seek to master others; to have a heart that is clean, a goal that is high; to learn to laugh yet never forget how to weep; to reach into the future yet never neglect the past; to be serious yet never to take yourself too seriously; to be modest so that you will remember the simplicity of true greatness, the open mind of true wisdom, the meekness of true strength.

They give you a temper of the will, a quality of the imagination, a vigor of the emotions, a freshness of the deep springs of life, a temperamental predominance of courage over timidity, an appetite for adventure over love of ease.

They create in your heart the sense of wonder, the unfailing hope of what next and the joy and inspiration of life. They teach you in this way to be an officer and a gentleman.

And what sort of soldiers are those you are to lead? Are they reliable, are they brave, are they capable of victory? Their story is known to all of you; it is the story of the American man-at-arms. My estimate of him was formed on the battlefield many years ago, and has never changed. I regarded him then as I regard him now—as one of the world's noblest figures, not only as one of the finest military characters, but also as one of the most stainless.

His name and fame are the birthright of every American citizen. In his youth and strength, his love and loyalty, he gave all that mortality can give. He needs no eulogy from me or from any other man. He has written his own history and written it in red on his enemy's breast.

But when I think of his patience under adversity, of his courage under fire and of his modesty in victory, I am filled with an emotion of admiration I cannot put into words. He belongs to history as furnishing one of the greatest examples of successful patriotism; he belongs to posterity as the instructor of future generations in the principles of liberty and freedom; he belongs to the present, to us, by his virtues and by his achievements.

In twenty campaigns, on a hundred battlefields, around a thousand campfires, I have witnessed that enduring fortitude, that patriotic self-abnegation and that invincible determination which have carved his status in the hearts of his people. From one end of the world to the other, he has drained deep the chalice of courage.

As I listened to those songs of the glee club, in memory's eye I could see those staggering columns of the First World War, bending under soggy packs, on many a weary march from dripping dusk to drizzling dawn, slogging ankle deep through the mire of shell-shocked roads, to form grimly for the attack, blue-lipped, covered with sludge and mud, chilled by the wind and rain, driving home to their objective and, for many, to the judgment seat of God.

I do not know the dignity of their birth, but I do know the glory of their death. They died unquestioning, uncomplaining, with faith in their hearts, and on their lips the hope that we would go on to victory. Always for them—Duty—Honor—Country; always their blood and sweat and tears as we sought the way and the light and the truth.

And twenty years after, on the other side of the globe, again the filth of murky foxholes, the stench of ghostly trenches, the slime of dripping dugouts; those broiling suns of relentless heat, those torrential rains of devastating storm, the loneliness and utter desolation of jungle trails, the bitterness of long separation from those they loved and cherished, the deadly pestilence of tropical disease, the horror of stricken areas of war; their resolute and determined defense, their swift and sure attack, their indomitable purpose, their complete and decisive victory—always victory—always through the bloody haze of their last reverberating shot, the vision of gaunt, ghastly men reverently following your password of Duty—Honor—Country.

The code which those words perpetrate embraces the highest moral laws and will stand the test of any ethics of philosophies ever promulgated for the uplift of mankind. Its requirements are for the things that are right, and its restraints are from the things that are wrong.

The soldier, above all other men, is required to practice the greatest act of religious training—sacrifice. In battle and in the face of danger and death, he discloses those divine attributes which his Maker gave when He created man in His own image. No physical courage and no brute instinct can take the place of the Divine help which alone can sustain him. However horrible the incidents of war may be, the soldier who is called upon to offer and to give his life for his country is the noblest development of mankind.

You now face a new world—a world of change. The thrust into outer space of the satellites, spheres and missiles marked the beginning of another epoch in the long story of mankind—the chapter of the space age.

We deal now not with things of this world alone but with the illimitable distances and as yet unfathomed mysteries of the universe. We are reaching out for a new and boundless frontier. We speak in strange terms: of harnessing the cosmic energy; of making winds and tides work for us; of creating unheard-of synthetic materials to supplement or even replace our old standard basics; of purifying sea water for our drink; of mining ocean floors for new fields of wealth and food; of disease preventatives to expand life into the hundreds of years; of controlling the weather for a more equitable distribution of heat and cold, of rain and shine; of space ships to the moon; of the primary target in war, no longer limited to the armed forces of an enemy, but instead to include his civil populations; of ultimate conflict between a united human race and the sinister forces of some other planetary galaxy; of such dreams and fantasies as to make life the most exciting of all time.

And through all this welter of change and development, your mission remains fixed, determined, inviolable—it is to win our wars. Everything else in your professional career is but a corollary to this vital dedication. All other public purposes, all other public projects, all other public needs, great or small, will find others for their accomplishment; but you are the ones who are trained to fight; yours is the profession of arms—the will to win, the sure knowledge that in war there is no substitute for victory; that if you lose, the nation will be destroyed; that the very obsession of your public service must be Duty—Honor—Country.

Others will debate the controversial issues, national and international, which divide men's minds; but serene, calm, aloof, you stand as the nation's war guardian, as its lifeguard from the raging tides of international conflict; as its gladiator in the arena of battle. For a century and a half, you have defended, guarded and protected its hallowed traditions of liberty and freedom, of right and justice.

Let civilian voices argue the merits or demerits of our processes of government; whether our strength is being sapped by deficit financing, indulged in too long; by federal paternalism grown too mighty; by power groups grown too arrogant; by politics grown too corrupt; by crime grown too rampant; by morals grown too low; by taxes grown too high; by extremists grown too violent; whether our personal liberties are as thorough and complete as they should be. These great national problems are not for your professional participation or military solution. Your guidepost stands out like a tenfold beacon in the night—Duty—Honor—Country.

You are the leaven which binds together the entire fabric of our national system of defense. From your ranks come the great captains who hold the nation's destiny in their hands the moment the war tocsin sounds. The Long Gray Line has never failed us. Were you to do so, a million ghosts in olive drab, in brown khaki, in blue and gray, would rise from their white crosses thundering those magic words—Duty—Honor—Country.

This does not mean that you are warmongers. On the contrary, the soldier, above all other people, prays for peace; for he must suffer and bear the deepest wounds and scars of war. But always in our ears ring the ominous words of Plato, that wisest of all philosophers, *"Only the dead have seen the end of war."*

The shadows are lengthening for me. The twilight is here. My days of old have vanished tone and tint; they have gone glimmering through the dreams of things that were. Their memory is one of wondrous beauty, watered by tears and coaxed and caressed by the smiles of yesterday.

I listen vainly, but with thirsty ear, for the witching melody of faint bugles blowing reveille, of far drums beating the long roll. In my dreams I hear again the crash of guns, the rattle of musketry, the strange mournful mutter of the battlefield.

But in the evening of my memory, always I come back to West Point. Always there echoes and re-echoes in my ears—Duty—Honor—Country.

Today marks my final roll call with you. But I want you to know that when I cross the river my last conscious thoughts will be of the Corps—and the Corps—and the Corps.

I bid you farewell.

This is...

AMERICA!

The freedom to worship God in the church of our choice.

The right to vote, and for whomever we please.

The right to give 'em a "piece of our mind," and still have a piece left.

Baseball with its peanuts, and taking a couple of digs at the umpire.

Here we can call the Governor "Pete," or don't have to call him at all. No doffing the cap or bending the knee.

Every man in his own right a king, his home his castle.

A breakfast of pancakes, sausage and maple syrup.

The good old country fairs.

The annual picnic where bank president and building janitor slap each other on the back.

No separate upper or lower berth for those of upper or lower birth.

Good old apple pie a la mode.

A steady job.

The best pay workers get anywhere in the world.

A car in which to go sightseeing around the country.

A good garden to plant and putter around in.

The happy thought that our sons can become famous.

THIS IS AMERICA!

—Adapted from *Railway Employees' Journal*

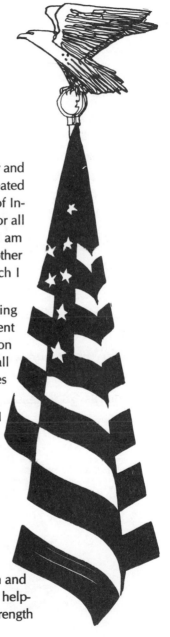

America's Message to the World

I am the United States. I was conceived in liberty and dedicated to the proposition that all men are created equal in the sight of God. I am the Declaration of Independence and the Constitution. I am freedom for all men. The blood of the world runs in my veins. I am over 3 1/2 million living people, and the voice of other millions who have died for the freedom for which I stand and which I still make possible.

I am sleepy, rustic villages and surging, roaring cities, fruitful vines and fertile fields, magnificent mountains and dry, dusty deserts. I am 3 1/2 million square miles, 4 1/2 million farms, 10 million small businesses. I am 200 thousand schools and colleges and 300 thousand churches.

I am Paul Revere's "The British are coming!" I am Patrick Henry's "Give me liberty or give me death!"

I am Washington in prayer at Valley Forge, Lincoln in sorrow at Gettysburg, MacArthur in return at Manila.

I am the Defender of freedom. In answer to its call, I left my heroic dead in Flanders Field, Pearl Harbor, Okinawa, Korea and Vietnam. I am the voice of freedom, and freedom is breath and my blood. Without it I'd die! And God willing and helping, may I always possess the integrity and inner strength

America's Message cont'd

of unity to keep myself unshackled and to remain forever the citadel of freedom, a beacon of hope to all men everywhere!

I am the American flag—13 stripes to remind all of my humble beginning and 50 white stars on a field of blue, showing the strength of unity with integrity, as captured in those immortal words of Lincoln, "The Union—at any price!" If you have ever known the feeling of seeing me unfurled over a stronghold of evil, stormed in the cause of right or waving proudly in the breeze in a foreign land to the stirring sound of "Retreat" or "Taps," then you know why men are willing to follow me and to die for the freedom for which I stand.

—Copied

LEIF ERIKSON made the first great journey of discovery in the year 1000—and reached America first. But that discovery was lost until October 12, 1492, when Christopher Columbus reached our shores—"Thanking God for His goodness and planting the sacred cross."

The Voyages of Columbus.

POCAHONTAS

(1595-1617), an Indian who helped maintain peace between English colonists and native Americans by befriend- ing the settlers and eventually marrying one of them.

— Pocahontas and Captain John Smith.

Daughter of a power- ful intertribal leader, Pocahontas first became acquainted with the col- onists in 1607. The following year, according to Capt. John Smith, founder and leader of the colony, she saved Smith's life after he had been captured by her father's tribe.

Pocahontas was the very first Indian convert in America. She was baptized at Jamestown.

THE PILGRIMS LANDED AT PLYMOUTH ROCK MASSACHUSETTS DECEMBER 21ST 1620

Then on a stormy day in the fall of 1620 the *Mayflower* with its 102 Pilgrims dropped anchor near present Plymouth, Massachusetts.

Our Pilgrim fathers had the spirit of Thanksgiving—and "thanksliving"—as they saw the hand of God in all everyday blessings. But nationally they did not set down their Ebenezer of praise until 1633, when they set apart a day to praise God from whom all blessings flowed. Later national dates of Thanksgiving have been in 1784—for declaration of peace and American independence—and when Lincoln declared a national Thanksgiving Day in 1863. Since then, every U. S. President has declared one.

May it not be an empty custom, but "in every thing give thanks; for this is the will of God in Christ Jesus concerning you."

*   *   *

We have forgotten God. We have forgotten the gracious hand which preserved us in peace and enriched and strengthened us; and we have vainly imagined that all things were produced by some superior wisdom and virtue of our own. Intoxicated with unbroken success, we have become too self-sufficient to feel the necessity of redeeming and preserving grace, too proud to pray to the God who made us.

—Abraham Lincoln

*   *   *

"The liberties of our country . . . are worth defending at all hazards; and it is our duty to defend them against all attacks. We have received them as fair inheritance from our worthy ancestors . . . [who] purchased them for us with toil and danger . . . . "

—Samuel Adams

The Pilgrims Land at Plymouth Rock 1620

Our American democracy rests on strong religious foundations. The Pilgrims who came to New England were fleeing from religious persecution. James I of England had warned them that, unless they conformed to the Anglican Church, he would "harrie them out of the land or else do worse."

After being persecuted by the State Church of England, they fled to Holland where their children were "in danger to degenerate and be corrupted," to lose their English speech and nationality and become Dutchmen. Accordingly, some of them decided it would be better to go, like "pilgrims," to America, the new lands across the seas. Here they could be missionaries to the heathen Indians. Here they could establish a government based on their religious ideas. Here they could found a little state for themselves.

We look back now to that momentous time in 1620 when those Bible-toting 102 Pilgrims boarded the *Mayflower* and set sail for a strange new world. Why? That they might worship and serve God freely.

After 9 weeks—do you know how long that is to be out on the rolling waves?—they landed at Plymouth, on the Massachusetts coast.

Plymouth Rock, as probably seen by the first Pilgrims

But before landing in the New World, they committed themselves to God's care. "Solemnly and mutually in the Presence of God and one of another," so the *Mayflower Compact* says, they set out to form a Christian community on the bleak New England shore.

They immediately set to work building shelters and preparing themselves for the cold winter, but they had trouble from the start. These people paid a big price for the privilege of worshiping God freely. Forty-four died before spring. Only 58 survived to plant the spring crops. But not a single Pilgrim returned to England with the *Mayflower*. "They had put their hand to the plough and did not look back."

But the Lord gave them courage, and that summer He gave them a good harvest. Governor Bradford proclaimed December 13 as a day of thanksgiving, and those Pilgrims gathered with about 80 friendly Indians for a celebration.

It was not a one-day event. They needed three days to express their thanksgiving. The *World Book Encyclopedia* says they devoted the time to preaching, praying, singing and then eating.

To them it meant more than a day of feasting and frolic, a meal of stuffed turkey followed by bicarbonate of soda and a football game. Thanksgiving Day was centered in the Lord, in singing hymns, reading the Scripture and giving thanks to God and enjoying the food God had provided.

"If you are not governed by God, you will be ruled by tyrants."

—William Penn, 1681

The Mayflower Compact

In the Name of God, Amen. We whose names are underwritten, the loyal subjects of our dread sovereign Lord, King James, by the grace of God, of Great Britain, France and Ireland King, Defender of the Faith, etc.,

Having undertaken, for the glory of God, and advancement of the Christian faith and honor of our King and Country, a voyage to plant the first colony in the northern parts of Virginia, do by these presents solemnly and mutually in the presence of God, and one of another, covenant and combine ourselves together into a civil body politic, for our better ordering and preservation and furtherance of the ends aforesaid; and by virtue hereof to enact, constitute and frame such just and equal laws, ordinances, acts, constitutions and offices, from time to time, as shall be thought most meet and convenient for the general good of the colony: unto which we promise all due submission and obedience.

In witness whereof we have hereunder subscribed our names at Cape Cod the *11 of November, in the year of the reign of our sovereign Lord, King James of England, France and Ireland the eighteenth, and of Scotland the fifty-fourth. Ano. Dom. 1620.

John Carver,	Richard Warren,	John Turner,	Edmond Margeson,
William Bradford,	John Howland,	Francis Eaton,	Peter Brown,
Edward Winslow,	Stephen Hopkins,	James Chilton,	Richard Britteridge,
William Brewster,	Edward Tilly,	John Crackston,	George Soule,
Isaac Allerton,	John Tilly,	John Billington,	Richard Clarke,
Myles Standish,	Francis Cooke,	Moses Fletcher,	Richard Gardiner,
John Alden,	Thomas Rogers,	John Goodman,	John Allerton,
Samuel Fuller,	Thomas Tinker,	Degory Priest,	Thomas English,
Christopher Martin,	John Rigdale,	Thomas Williams,	Edward Doty,
William Mullins,	Edward Fuller,	Gilbert Winslow,	Edward Leister
William White,			

*Old calendar

Thanks to God

Thanks to God for my Redeemer,
Thanks for all Thou dost provide!
Thanks for times now but a mem'ry,
Thanks for Jesus by my side!
Thanks for pleasant, balmy springtime,
Thanks for dark and dreary fall!
Thanks for tears by now forgotten,
Thanks for peace within my soul!

Thanks for prayers that Thou hast answered,
Thanks for what Thou dost deny!
Thanks for storms that I have weathered,
Thanks for all Thou dost supply!
Thanks for pain and thanks for pleasure,
Thanks for comfort in despair!
Thanks for grace that none can measure,
Thanks for love beyond compare!

Thanks for roses by the wayside,
Thanks for thorns their stems contain!
Thanks for home and thanks for fireside,
Thanks for hope, that sweet refrain!
Thanks for joy and thanks for sorrow,
Thanks for heav'nly peace with Thee!
Thanks for hope in the tomorrow,
Thanks through all eternity!

—J. A. Hultman
Translated C. E. Backstrom

Think of that little band of people who crossed the Atlantic in a sailboat that measured 26 x 113 feet and landed on the New England coast during a bitter cold winter. At times that first year the daily ration of those who were well was only five grains of corn. During the first five months in America, half of their number died and were buried by night in unmarked graves so the Indians would not know their numbers were being depleted.

After suffering every conceivable hardship, they had a harvest of 21 acres of corn in the fall of 1621 and immediately offered thanks to God for His blessings. The little group, led by Governor William Bradford, marched triumphantly through the cornfields singing, "The earth is the Lord's and the fullness thereof, the world and they that dwell therein." They sat down to a meal in gladness and joy, giving gratitude to God who made it all possible.

The very lives of the people were centered around God's Word. In their homes they read, reread and meditated upon the sacred Book. Their schools had as their only textbook the Bible.

"Give Me Liberty or Give Me Death"

By PATRICK HENRY

Delivered on March 23,1775, before the Second Revolutionary Convention of Virginia, in the old church in Richmond.

No man thinks more highly than I do of the patriotism, as well as abilities, of the very worthy gentlemen who have just addressed the House. But different men often see the same subject in different lights; therefore, I hope it will not be thought disrespectful to those gentlemen if, entertaining as I do opinions of a character very opposite to theirs, I shall speak forth my sentiments freely and without reserve. This is no time for ceremony.

The question before the House is one of awful moment to this country. For my own part, I consider it as nothing less than a question of freedom or slavery; and in proportion to the magnitude of the subject ought to be the freedom of the debate. It is only in this way that we can hope to arrive at truth and fulfil the great responsibility which we hold to God and our country. Should I keep back my opinions at such a time, through fear of giving offense, I should consider myself as guilty of treason toward my country and of an act of disloyalty toward the Majesty of Heaven, which I revere above all earthly kings.

Mr. President, it is natural to man to indulge in the illusions of hope. We are apt to shut our eyes against a painful truth and listen to the song of that siren, till she transforms us into beasts. Is this the part of wise men, engaged in a great and arduous struggle for liberty? Are we disposed to be of the number of those who, having eyes, see not, and having ears, hear not, the things which so nearly concern their temporal salvation?

For my part, whatever anguish of spirit it may cost, I am willing to know the whole truth, to know the worst, and to provide for it.

I have but one lamp by which my feet are guided, and that is the lamp of experience. I know of no way of judging of the future but by the past. And judging by the past, I wish to know what there has been in the conduct of the British ministry for the last ten years to justify those hopes with which gentlemen have been pleased to solace themselves and the House.

Is it that insidious smile with which our petition has been lately received? Trust it not, sir; it will prove a snare to your feet. Suffer not yourselves to be betrayed with a kiss. Ask yourselves how this gracious reception of our petition comports with those warlike preparations which cover our waters and darken our land.

Are fleets and armies necessary to a work of love and reconciliation? Have we shown ourselves so unwilling to be reconciled that force must be called in to win back our love?

Let us not deceive ourselves, sir. These are the implements of war and subjugation; the last arguments to which kings resort.

I ask gentlemen, sir, what means this martial array, if its purpose be not to force us to submission? Can gentlemen assign any other possible motive for it? Has Great Britain any enemy in this quarter of the world to call for all this accumulation of navies and armies?

No, sir, she has none. They are meant for us: they can be meant for no other. They are sent over to bind and rivet upon us those chains which the British ministry have been so long forging.

And what have we to oppose to them? Shall we try argument? Sir, we have been trying that for the last ten years. Have we anything new to offer upon the subject? Nothing. We have held the subject up in every light of which it is capable; but it has been all in vain.

Shall we resort to entreaty and humble supplication? What terms shall we find which have not been already exhausted? Let us not, I beseech you, sir, deceive ourselves longer. Sir, we have done everything that could be done, to avert the storm which is now coming on. We have petitioned; we have remonstrated; we have supplicated; we have prostrated ourselves before the throne, and have implored its interposition to arrest the tyrannical hands of the ministry and Parliament. Our petitions have been slighted; our remonstrances have produced additional violence and insult; our supplications have been disregarded, and we have been spurned, with contempt, from the foot of the throne!

In vain, after these things, may we indulge the fond hope of peace and reconciliation. There is no longer any room for hope. If we wish to be free—if we mean to preserve inviolate those inestimable privileges for which we have been so long contending—if we mean not basely to abandon the noble struggle in which we have been so long engaged and which we have pledged ourselves never to abandon until the glorious object of our contest shall be obtained—we must fight! I repeat it, sir, we must fight! An appeal to arms and to the God of Hosts is all that is left us!

They tell us, sir, that we are weak—unable to cope with so formidable an adversary. But when shall we be stronger? Will it be the next week, or the next year? Will it be when we are totally disarmed, and when a British guard shall be stationed in every house?

Shall we gather strength by irresolution and inaction? Shall we acquire the means of effectual resistance by lying supinely on our backs and hugging the delusive phantom of hope, until our enemies shall have bound us hand and foot?

Sir, we are not weak if we make a proper use of those means which the God of nature has placed in our power. Three millions of people armed in the holy cause of liberty, and in such a country as that which we possess, are invincible by any force which our enemy can send against us.

Besides, sir, we shall not fight our battles alone. There is a just God who presides over the destinies of nations and who will raise up friends to fight our battles for us.

The battle, sir, is not to the strong alone; it is to the vigilant, the active, the brave. Besides, sir, we have no election. It we were base enough to desire it, it is now too late to retire from the contest. There is no retreat but in submission and slavery!

Our chains are forged! Their clanking may be heard on the plains of Boston! The war is inevitable—and let it come! I repeat it, sir, let it come!

It is in vain, sir, to extenuate the matter. Gentlemen may cry, "Peace, Peace"—but there is no peace. The war is actually begun! The next gale that sweeps from the north will bring to our ears the clash of resounding arms! Our brethren are already in the field!

Why stand we here idle? What is it that gentlemen wish? What would they have? Is life so dear, or peace so sweet, as to be purchased at the price of chains and slavery? Forbid it, Almighty God! I know not what course others may take, but as for me, give me liberty or give me death!

(William Wirt, the biographer of Henry, says that when Henry took his seat, "no murmur of applause was heard. The effect was too deep. After the trance of a moment, several members started from their seats. The cry to arms seemed to quiver on every lip and gleam from every eye. They became impatient of speech. Their souls were on fire for action.")

*   *   *

It is said that in the will of Patrick Henry, who made the above celebrated speech before the Revolutionary War, there was the following paragraph:

I have now disposed of all my property to my family. There is one thing more that I wish I could give to them. That is the Christian religion. If they had that and I had not given them one shilling, they would have been rich; and if they had not that and I had given them the world, they would be poor.

PAUL REVERE (1735-1818)...

folk hero of the American Revolution whose dramatic horseback ride on the night of April 18, 1775, warning Boston-area residents that the British were coming, was immortalized in a ballad by Henry Wadsworth Longfellow.

In the 1770s Revere immersed himself in the movement toward political independence from Great Britain. In 1773 he donned Indian garb and joined 50 other patriots in the Boston Tea Party protest against parliamentary taxation without representation.

Although many have questioned the historical liberties taken in Longfellow's narrative poem, the fact is that the legendary figure served for years as the principal rider for Boston's Committee of Safety, making journeys to New York and Philadelphia in its service.

On April 16, 1775, he rode to nearby Concord to urge the patriots to move their military stores, endangered by pending British troop movements. Finally, two days later, he set out on his most famous journey to alert his countrymen that the redcoats were on the march, particularly in search of Revolutionary leaders John Hancock and Samuel Adams. Because of his warning, the Minutemen were ready the next morning on Lexington green for the historic battle that launched the War of Independence.

Paul Revere's Ride

Listen, my children, and you shall hear
Of the midnight ride of Paul Revere,
On the eighteenth of April, in Seventy-five;
Hardly a man is now alive
Who remembers that famous day and year.

He said to his friend, "If the British march
By land or sea from the town tonight,
Hang a lantern aloft in the belfry arch
Of the North Church tower as a signal light,—
One, if by land, and two, if by sea;
And I on the opposite shore will be,
Ready to ride and spread the alarm
Through every Middlesex village and farm,
For the country folk to be up and to arm."

**Paul Revere rides after seeing signal in tower of
Old North Church, Boston, on April 18, 1775.**

Then he said, "Good night!" and with muffled oar
Silently rowed to the Charlestown shore,
Just as the moon rose over the bay,
Where swinging wide at her moorings lay
The Somerset, British man-of-war;
A phantom ship, with each mast and spar
Across the moon like a prison bar,
And a huge black hulk, that was magnified
By its own reflection in the tide.

Meanwhile, his friend, through alley and street,
Wanders and watches with eager ears,
Till in the silence around him he hears
The muster of men at the barrack door,
The sound of arms, and the tramp of feet,
And the measured tread of the grenadiers,
Marching down to their boats on the shore.

Then he climbed the tower of the Old North Church,
By the wooden stairs, with stealthy tread,
To the belfry-chamber overhead,
And startled the pigeons from their perch
On the sombre rafters, that round him made
Masses and moving shapes of shade,—
By the trembling ladder, steep and tall,
To the highest window in the wall,
Where he paused to listen and look down
A moment on the roofs of the town,
And the moonlight flowing over all.

Beneath, in the churchyard, lay the dead,
In their night-encampment on the hill,
Wrapped in silence so deep and still
That he could hear, like a sentinel's tread,
The watchful night-wind, as it went
Creeping along from tent to tent,
And seeming to whisper, "All is well!"
A moment only he feels the spell
Of the place and the hour, and the secret dread
Of the lonely belfry and the dead;
For suddenly all his thoughts are bent
On a shadowy something far away,
Where the river widens to meet the bay,—
A line of black that bends and floats
On the rising tide, like a bridge of boats.

Meanwhile, impatient to mount and ride,
Booted and spurred, with a heavy stride
On the opposite shore walked Paul Revere.
Now he patted his horse's side,
Now gazed at the landscape far and near,
Then, impetuous, stamped the earth,
And turned and tightened his saddlegirth;
But mostly he watched with eager search
The belfry-tower of the Old North Church,
As it rose above the graves on the hill,
Lonely and spectral and sombre and still.
And lo! as he looks, on the belfry's height
A glimmer, and then a gleam of light!
He springs to the saddle, the bridle he turns,
But lingers and gazes, till full on his sight
A second lamp in the belfry burns!

A hurry of hoofs in a village street,
A shape in the moonlight, a bulk in the dark,
And beneath, from the pebbles, in passing a spark
Struck out by a steed flying fearless and fleet:
That was all! And yet, through the gloom and the light,
The fate of a nation was riding that night;
And the spark struck out by that steed, in his flight,
Kindled the land into flame with its heat.

He has left the village and mounted the steep,
And beneath him, tranquil and broad and deep,
Is the Mystic, meeting the ocean tides;
And under the alders that skirt its edge,
Now soft on the sand, now loud on the ledge,
Is heard the tramp of his steed as he rides.

It was twelve by the village clock,
When he crossed the bridge into Medford town.
He heard the crowing of the cock,
And the barking of the farmer's dog,
And felt the damp of the river fog,
That rises after the sun goes down.

It was one by the village clock,
When he galloped into Lexington.
He saw the gilded weathercock
Swim in the moonlight as he passed,

And the meeting-house windows, blank and bare,
Gaze at him with a spectral glare,
As if they already stood aghast
At the bloody work they would look upon.

It was two by the village clock,
When he came to the bridge in Concord town.
He heard the bleating of the flock,
And the twitter of birds among the trees,
And felt the breath of the morning breeze
Blowing over the meadows brown.
And one was safe and asleep in his bed
Who at the bridge would be first to fall,
Who that day would be lying dead,
Pierced by a British musket-ball.

You know the rest. In the books you have read,
How the British Regulars fired and fled,—
How the farmers gave them ball for ball,
From behind each fence and farm-yard wall,
Chasing the red-coats down the lane,
Then crossing the fields to emerge again
Under the trees at the turn of the road,
And only pausing to fire and load.

So through the night rode Paul Revere;
And so through the night went his cry of alarm
To every Middlesex village and farm,—
A cry of defiance and not of fear,
A voice in the darkness, a knock at the door,
And a word that shall echo forevermore!
For, borne on the night-wind of the Past,
Through all our history, to the last,
Is the hour of darkness and peril and need,
The people will waken and listen to hear
The hurrying hoofbeats of that steed,
And the midnight message of Paul Revere.

—Henry Wadsworth Longfellow

THE OLD NORTH CHURCH OF BOSTON . . . played a prominent part in history. Well preserved, it has been a landmark for over 200 years. It had a most important part in the early struggle of the colonists to throw off the chains of oppression. After 7 years of revolt, freedom and independence were attained, the new nation was formed.

Christ Church was its name, but it was better known as the Old North Church. On its northly side, near the top of a hill, is one of those old colonial burial grounds, surrounded by a pointed iron fence.

The church is a brick structure with a square brick tower and a high wooden steeple. It faces north and overlooks Boston harbor and the Charlestown shore. It is a duplicate of a famous church built by Christopher Wren that stood in London for centuries but blitzed out in World War II.

The chancel at the front has the Lord's Prayer, the Apostles' Creed and the 23rd Psalm in large gold lettering. In the back is a large balcony where the organ is located. When a hymn is sung, the congregation rises and faces the rear.

Tourists stop at Revere Mall in the rear, climb the outside steps, enter the side door, pass through the office and find their seats. The lecturer gives a 5-minute talk, telling how on the night of April 18, 1775, the British force went by water and the sexton slowly and cautiously climbed the darkened stairs that lead to the belfry, brushed aside the cobwebs and hung out the two lanterns as the pre-arranged signal to Paul Revere, waiting with his saddled horse. He mounted and was on his way to deliver the message, and the rest is history which you know.

After hanging the lanterns the sexton warily descended and escaped through the window avoiding the British patrol keeping watch to pick up any suspicious characters prowling about. The sexton fled to Hingham where he remained until the British evacuated Boston.

Battle of Bunker Hill . . .

was fought June 17, 1775, the first great battle of the Revolution. Americans, under Dr. Joseph Warren, built a redoubt on nearby Breed's Hill, where the battle actually occurred, in order to defend Boston. British troops assaulted the hill and were repulsed twice. They succeeded in their third attempt, sustaining heavy losses. Legend tells that as the last assault began, the Americans (their powder nearly gone) were ordered by Col. William Prescott, *"Don't fire until you see the whites of their eyes!"*

Crossing the Delaware

After numerous and tragic defeats for the Continental Army, General Washington planned one of the most daring attacks of the Revolution. On Christmas night, 1776, under the worst possible conditions, he loaded three divisions in rowboats to cross the Delaware River. Only one division reached the New Jersey shore, but the Hessian forces at Trenton were caught unaware and quickly surrendered. The Americans lost only two men. This brilliant victory at Trenton, and another only days later at Princeton, were electrical, reviving the hopes of the nation.

1776 and METHODISM

Francis Asbury was one of a number of preachers John Wesley sent to America to preach the Methodist doctrine of salvation from all sin.

When the American Revolution broke out, all the Methodists went home except one—Francis Asbury. The American Revolution was not an easy time for American Methodism. It was in its beginning stages and not separated from its mother, the Anglican Church. John Wesley, the leader of the Methodist movement, was very English. Wesley published a pamphlet deriding the colonies for their lack of loyalty to the English crown. How could there be such an agitation for liberty? Some of those advocating freedom were slave owners. Needless to say, Mr. Wesley's pamphlet reached Francis Asbury in a most inopportune time.

Coming to America, Francis Asbury was responding to a sense of the divine call. In England he had been a Methodist preacher for some five years, but in the annual meeting of the preachers, 1771, Wesley asked for volunteers to serve in the colonies and Asbury was one of the two accepted. He was twenty-six years of age when he came to the New World. He placed his hand upon the plow and never looked back. He wrote, *"My heart melted within me to think from whence I came, where I was going and where I was going about. I feel that God is here."*

Asbury had been devoutly religious from his youthful days, growing up in Hansworth near Birmingham. He was the son of a gardener for a well-to-do family. He was awakened at the age of thirteen during a time of prayer. *"The Lord pardoned my sins,"* he testified, *"and justified my soul."*

From the age of sixteen he began taking a leadership role and then preaching in Methodist meetings in that area. At the age of twenty-one he was accepted as one of Wesley's preachers who did not have to be ordained or have a college education. He received a circuit assignment. He was a man of incessant activity. His dedication to God and the cause of full salvation was complete.

Instead of settling down in New York or Philadelphia to come to a comfortable circuit, he took to the wilderness roads teaching and preaching the Gospel of salvation. Asbury shook up the clergy and insisted they get out and ride the circuits. One year after he arrived in America, Mr. Wesley appointed him to head the work in the colonies.

Right after the War of Revolution, Wesley sent Thomas Coke with instruction that he and Asbury should work together as superintendents. Coke ordained Asbury, December 27, 1784. Some time after the arrival of Coke, two American superintendents appointed by Wesley started using the title of Bishop, a tradition that continues to this day in the United States. Wesley was frankly shocked, horrified and revolted. He wrote, ''Men may call me a naive or a fool or a rascal or a scoundrel and I am content, but my dear Frankie, we shall never by my consent call me Bishop.''

Asbury rejected Wesley's advice concerning responsibility as well as the title of Bishop, feeling that Wesley was too far away to properly evaluate circumstances in the colony.

Coke stayed in America only a few months and then returned home, making an occasional visit. This left Asbury in full command of the work. He never returned to England. He never married. He never established a home. He was too busy riding the American circuit, some

5,000 miles on horseback a year. He continued this practice until 1816
when he went to be with His Lord. He was so well known in the colonies
that a letter from England had only to be addressed to The Reverend Bishop
Asbury, North America, and it would reach him. He was totally dedicated
to God, a man with a single mind which at times is not easy to get along
with. He spoke plainly and closely to the people.

When the preachers grumbled, he insisted they take their assignments
in spite of what might be bothering them. He always did more than he
asked anyone else to do and he was always examining his own heart plainly
and closely. The result was a system of circuit-riding preachers across
the backwoods of America until there was hardly a crossroads or a
backwoods clearing that did not see the Methodist preacher riding by, stopping to kindle the spiritual flame. "There is nobody out tonight but crows
and Methodist preachers" was a saying in bad weather.

His movements were restricted during the time of the American Revolution. He refused to take the loyalty oath in Maryland and found refuge
in Delaware where preachers were not required to take an oath. He spent
considerable time during the Revolution in reading and writing as well
as praying. He wrote in July 1776, "My present mode of conduct is as
follows: To read about 100 pages a day, usually to pray in public five
times a day, to preach in the open air every other day and to lecture in
prayer meeting each evening."

In March of 1778, he confided to his diary, "I was under some heaviness
of mind, but it was no wonder—3,000 miles from home, my friends have
left me and I am considered by some an enemy of the country, every day
liable to be seized by violence and abuse. However, all of this is but a
trifle to suffer for Christ and the salvation of souls. Lord stand by me."

He took up residence with a Judge Thomas White near Dover and stayed
there most of the next two years; however, the judge was arrested at his
home and held for some time. Asbury left and found another place to stay
but received warnings of further danger. Accordingly he writes, "I set
out after dinner and lay in a swamp until sunset. I was then kindly taken
in by a friend." In less than a month he was back at White's and stayed
there until the patriots came to realize that Asbury posed no danger and
let him travel freely again.

It is impossible to estimate the tremendous work of this itinerate preacher.

In 1780 Asbury wrote to Wesley, "Many in the north and some in the south are daily coming home to God. We have upwards of 80 traveling preachers and nearly 15,000 members."

When he came to America there were only 1,000 American Methodists. When he died in 1816 over 200,000 people at that time bore the name of Methodist. A revolution had taken place under the leadership of this quiet, gentle, Christlike man. He carried no sword but a Bible. He held no office but that of Bishop. He did not carry the prestige of Washington, Adams or Jefferson, but nevertheless he carried the blessing and glory of God. He carried the good news of salvation to a wilderness world and the wild colonial revolutionaries and brought them into captivity to Jesus Christ.

He and his Methodist preachers changed the religious landscape of America.

—From the Editor of *Convention Herald*

The Circuit-riding Preacher

Stories of pony express riders, prospectors, sheriffs and cattlemen abound in the recorded history of America's Westward expansion. Another group, equally important though less often commemorated in legend, are the circuit-riding preachers who took the Word of God into the frontier and blazed the trail for Christianity in the wilderness.

The circuit-riding preacher had no established church, set worship times or permanent congregation. Instead, he preached anywhere he happened to be, on almost every day of the week, to anyone who would listen. Thus, a circuit rider could be found holding a service in a log cabin, tavern or under a shade tree.

Since his circuit was usually large and his time in any one place short, the circuit rider would appoint "class leaders" at various locations to conduct Bible studies after he had gone on to another settlement.

The circuit system, devised by Wesley, had Methodist begin-

nings in England. It was introduced into America by Francis Asbury. Baptists and Presbyterians also used circuit riders, but the Methodists were most successful.

The first regularly appointed American circuit rider was sent over the Allegheny Mountains to the wilderness in 1782. In 1784 the Redstone circuit was established in southwestern Pennsylvania. By 1789, there were ten Methodist circuits—four in Tennessee, three in Kentucky, and three along the upper Ohio River.

By the end of the eighteenth century, there were 2,000 Methodists in Kentucky and Tennessee alone, largely because of the circuit riders' work.

Thus, though he has not been the hero of many books and films, the circuit-riding preacher made his mark. As the bearer of God's good news, he was instrumental in determining how the Bible shaped America.

* * *

PATRIOTISM

by Susan Coolidge

He serves his country best
Who lives pure life and doeth righteous deed,
And walks straight paths however others stray,
And leaves his sons, as uttermost bequest,
A stainless record which all men may read;
  This is the better way.

No drop but serves the slowly lifting tide;
No dew but has an errand to some flower;
No smallest star but sheds some helpful ray,
And man by man, each helping all the rest,
Make the firm bulwark of the country's power;
  There is no better way.

Spreading the Gospel

The history of modern missions runs parallel to that of the United States. Early discoverers and explorers of the American continents were motivated not only to claim territory but also to bring the Christian message to the New World.

At this time it was considered a governmental responsibility to spread the Christian faith. Not until later did the Christian church once more assume its God-given role in missionary outreach.

Missions interest was already evident in the colonies before independence. Individuals such as Jonathan Edwards preached to the American Indians. In **1762** a missionary society was chartered in Massachusetts. However, it was disallowed by the king and was short-lived.

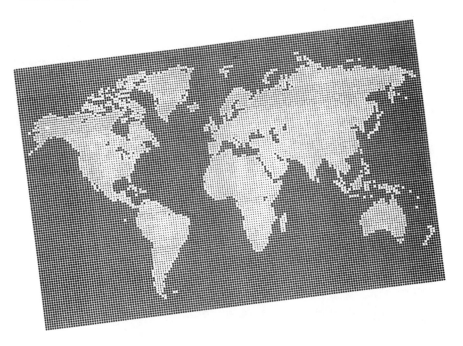

After independence was declared in **1776**, missions became an integral part of national development. Through the years, as our country continued to develop, interest in missions grew.

1787—First American missions societies are formed to reach the frontier settlements, the American Indians, and the heathen overseas. But the enormous needs of the expanding frontier absorb all of their energy.

1790—Moravians undertake missionary work among the Indian population of New York and Pennsylvania. (Their success undoubtedly influenced later missions outreaches from North America.)

1793—The era of modern missions begins. In June, Englishman William Carey goes to India. His booklet, *An Inquiry Into the Obligations of Christians to Use Means for the Conversion of the Heathen,* greatly influences the missions activity beginning in North America.

1810—The American Board of Commissioners for Foreign Missions (Congregational) forms and directs its first missions work from North America. (This board resulted from the "haystack" group—students at Williams College, Williamstown, Massachusetts, who met to pray for the lost. They were dubbed the "haystack" group after a sudden rain interrupted their prayer meeting and they took refuge under a haystack.)

1812—Adoniram Judson, the first missionary sent out from North America, goes to Burma.

1819—The first medical missionary, Dr. John Scudder, is sent to India by an American board. This is the start of a long line of missionary succession in this famous family.

1835—American Baptists send to India their first missionary, Nathan Brown.

1840-1860—More mission boards form. Volunteers for service are forthcoming spontaneously in abundance.

1866—The Student Volunteer Movement at Mt. Hermon, Massachusetts, is sparked by Evangelist D. L. Moody at the Northfield Conference. This is the beginning of the World Student Christian Movement.

1882 Nyack Missionary College in Nyack, New York, is founded by A. B. Simpson. (This college is now a school of theology and missions under the Christian and Missionary Alliance.)

OUR AMERICAN HERITAGE

MRS. DOROTHY WALTERS

The role of Judeo-Christianity has been a major influence in the United States since the Pilgrim Fathers landed at Plymouth Rock. The Mayflower Compact begins with the words, "In the name of God, Amen . . . ."

In 1835, a French visitor to the United States made this comment: "Upon my arrival, the religious aspect of the country was the first thing that struck my attention. I do not know if all Americans have a sincere faith in their religion, but I am certain that they hold it indispensible to the maintenance of republican institutions."

Other people have marveled at the Judeo-Christian belief that does not stem from some manmade idea, but it is written indelibly into the laws of nature by God. No other nation in the world has so many declarations of allegiance to God, dependence upon His guidance, and appeals to a "Supreme Judge" in order to build a new Nation.

The idea of freedom as the right of all men takes us back to the creation of man whom God made in His own likeness, making him free to roam the earth and decide if he would serve his Creator. Many of the prophets proclaimed liberty—God's endowed right of freedom— even in the face of kings. Moses dared the wrath of King Pharaoh by demanding that he "Let my people go!" and led Israel into a country where they would be free to worship God. God gave them a Jubilee day of atonement to ". . . proclaim liberty throughout all the land unto all the inhabitants thereof. . ." (Lev. 25:10). Later on, yes, many centuries later, these words were inscribed on America's Liberty Bell.

Liberty and freedom were the words the church cast again and again, "We must obey God rather than man." The tyrants did not fear the Christian's piety, but they feared this idea of the freedom of God's people.

It was in the pursuit of this ideal of freedom that a group of brave men, women and children climbed aboard a little ship called the "Mayflower," and with only their Bibles and a dream of liberty they landed in America in 1620. The Puritans who followed gave their reasons for coming to America in the opening sequence of their New England Confederation by these words: "We all came into these parts of America with one and the same aim and end, namely, to advance the kingdom of the Lord Jesus Christ."

In the year of 1607, thirteen years before either of these two groups had arrived in America, a ship loaded with people from England landed at Cape Henry, Virginia, set up a cross, and held the first prayer meeting recorded in the history of America. A proclamation was made in England by Lord Delaware and others, claiming the land of Virginia for Jesus Christ and the glory of God.

When Roger Williams ran from the wrath of King Charles, he came to the Massachusetts Bay Colony in 1631, declaring religious freedom and separation of church and state. When he was rejected there, he fled to Providence, Rhode Island, and introduced religious freedom there—not only for Christians, but for Jews as well.

William Penn who had been in prison in England, when freed, led his Quaker Friends into New Jersey and what is now the state of Pennsylvania and drew up a frame of government which contained a bill of rights that emphasized religious freedom.

Others who came for the same purpose were the Dutch, Swedes, Germans, Moravians, Hugenots and Scots. These people established their religious beliefs from Manhattan Island and along the Delaware into the middle colonies. From this came men like John Adams who wrote, "Statesmen may plan and speculate for liberty, but it is religion and morality alone which freedom can securely stand."

In every area of American life "The Faith of Our Fathers" has left its imprint. The first schools in America used the Holy Bible as their first textbook. The churches founded the first institution of higher learning. The Declaration of Independence reflects the feelings of men to whom spirituality was all-important. The Declaration's giant step was being taken; they affirmed "with firm reliance upon the protection of Divine Providence."

There were many other great men who contributed much to our American heritage; among them, Francis Asbury. Born in England in 1745, he was an ardent follower of the evangelical preacher and founder of Methodism, John Wesley.

In 1771 Wesley sent Asbury to America as a missionary. He was only 22 years of age when he began the circuit-riding type of preaching originated by Wesley. He applied it with great success in the colonies. His ministry lasted 44 years, and he traveled on horseback a total of 300,000 miles. He had no home of his own but was a welcome guest wherever he went. In 1785 Francis Asbury became the first Bishop of the Methodist Episcopal Church and saw the church grow from 500 followers to 200,000. He ordained 3,000 circuit riders, and they were so faithful that a common remark during stormy weather was, "There's nothing out today but crows and Methodist preachers."

In 1871 French sculptor Frederic Bartholdi conceived the idea of a Statue that would commemorate both U. S. independence and France's own revolution. His vision of a colossal figure to be called "Liberty enlightening the world" was enthusiastically endorsed on both sides of the Atlantic. "Miss Liberty" was officially unveiled in New York Harbor on October 8, 1886, in a ceremony presided over by President Grover Cleveland. As the tide of emigration rose in the next decade, the 151-foot statue came to represent the gateway to the new world to millions of awed newcomers. Engraved on a bronze plaque on the statue's pedestal is the poem written by Emma Lazarus:

> Give me your tired, your poor,
> Your huddled masses yearning to breathe free.
> The wretched refuse of your teeming shore—
> Send these, the homeless, tempest-tost to me.
> I lift my lamp beside the golden door.

This year, 1988, we are celebrating the 212th anniversary of our government. We are a different people today than we were 212 years ago. Our society is more complex, more demanding, more pluralistic. We have fallen from the goals set by the originators of the Constitution of the United States. Many people in America have embraced communism, some of our national government heads have become dishonest and untrustworthy, and our country has lost its image to many other nations of the world; but overall the United States is still a free country under God and the greatest country in the world.

God hasn't changed, and He is still reigning and ruling in the affairs of men and nations. The goal of the born-again believers of America should be a return to "the Faith of Our Fathers." To do this we must resolve our prejudices and unite to restore the foundations that this great country were founded on. This can be backed up by the words of Solomon: "If my people, which are called by my name, shall humble themselves, and pray, and seek my face, and turn from their wicked ways; then will I hear from heaven, and will forgive their sin, and will heal their land" (II Chron. 7:14).

WHOM SHALL I SEND?

Whom shall I send? The voice of Jesus calls us;
O who will go to far-off lands of night,
Where dying souls, enslaved by sin, beseech us
For help, for hope, for freedom and for light?
Who, who will go, the Word of Life to take them,
Tell them of Christ, His mercy and His might?

I hear Thy call: as Lord and King I own Thee;
My lips have breathed Thy healing, holy Name;
Shall I delay for other hearts to heed Thee
While souls despair in sorrow and in shame?
Should Christ return before His Word has reached them,
How shall I bear the burden of my blame?

Lord, here am I—to go where Thou wilt send me,
To bear abroad the Name that makes men free;
Speak Thou through me the truth Thy grace has taught me;
Use my poor life to turn men's hearts to Thee!
I heed Thy call: the life I owe I bring Thee:
Lord, here am I—my Saviour, O send me!

—E. Margaret Clarkson

I Am the United States

I was born on July 4, 1776, and the Declaration of Independence is my birth certificate. The bloodlines of the world run in my veins, because I offered freedom to the oppressed. I am the United States.

I am the 180 million living souls, and the ghost of millions who have lived and died for me.

I am Nathan Hale and Paul Revere. I stood at Lexington and fired the shot heard round the world. I am Washington, Jefferson and Patrick Henry. I am John Paul Jones, the Green Mountain Boys and Davy Crockett. I am Lee, Grant and Abe Lincoln.

I am the Brooklyn Bridge, the wheat lands of Kansas and the granite hills of Vermont. I am the coal fields of the Virginias and Pennsylvania; the fertile lands of the West; the Golden Gate and the Grand Canyon. I am Independence Hall, the Monitor and the Merrimac.

I am big. I sprawl from the Atlantic to the Pacific, three million square miles throbbing with industry. I am more than five million farms. I am forest, field, mountain and desert. I am quiet villages and cities that never sleep. You can look at me and see Ben Franklin walking down the streets of Philadelphia with his bread loaf under his arm. You can see Betsy Ross with her needle. You can see the lights of Christmas, and hear the strains of "Auld Lang Syne" as the calendar turns.

I am Babe Ruth and the World Series. I am 169,000 schools and colleges and 250,000 churches where people worship God as they think best. I am a ballot dropped in a box; the roar of a crowd in a stadium, and the voice of a choir in a cathedral. I am an editorial in a newspaper and a letter to a Congressman.

I am Eli Whitney and Stephen Foster. I am Tom Edison, Albert Einstein and Billy Graham. I am Horace Greeley, Will Rogers and the Wright brothers. I am George Washington Carver, Daniel Webster and Jonas Salk.

I am Longfellow, Harriet Beecher Stowe, Walt Whitman, Thomas Paine.

Yes, I am the Nation, and these are the things that I am. I was conceived in freedom, and, God willing, in freedom will I spend the rest of my days. May I possess always the integrity, the courage and the strength to keep myself unshackled, to remain a citadel of freedom and a beacon of hope to the world.

I am the United States.

—Author Unknown
(from *The Arrowhead*)

Establishment 1776!

MELVIN MUNN, LIFE LINE Commentator

The men who signed the Declaration of Independence were mostly men of comfortable or rich means.

Each had far more to lose from revolution than he had to gain. It was principle, not property, which brought such men to Philadelphia to sign the Declaration.

They were of the Establishment, Style 1776. Had you been sent out to arrest some rebels, the chances are you would never have looked a second time at any of these men. Almost all of them had an abundant supply of fortune and sacred honor. When they pledged these to the support of a declaration that the Colonies would no longer be subservient to a distant king, a British fleet was already lying at anchor in New York Harbor.

Most of them were relatively young men, with enough worldly goods to be called affluent, but it was honor that motivated them most.

Benjamin Franklin was the only man among them who was really aged. Eighteen Founding Fathers were still less than 40 years old and three of them were still in their 20s. Their occupations were varied. Twenty-four were jurists or lawyers, 9 were landowners or rich farmers, and 11 were merchants. The rest were physicians, ministers, politicians and shippers. A few would have been called poor. Sam Adams of Massachusetts, the poorest, came to Congress wearing a new suit which had been given him by people who wished him well. He could not afford to buy one.

All but two who signed the Declaration had families, and most of them were men of education and considerable standing in their communities. Each came from what is now called the "power structure" of his area. Each enjoyed a security known to few men at that time.

These men of the 1776 Establishment knew the penalty for treason was death by hanging. Affixing their names to the Declaration of Independence was treason against His Majesty's government in London.

John Hancock inherited a great fortune, and there was already a price of 500 pounds on his head before the Declaration was accepted. You will recall the Hancock signature is the largest at the bottom of the document. He signed it in those huge letters so that in his words, "His Majesty could now read my name without glasses and could now double the reward."

The gallows was a favorite subject of humor at the signing. Benjamin Franklin said: "Indeed, we must all hang together, or assuredly we shall all hang separately." Then there was heavyweight Benjamin Harrison of Virginia who told diminutive Elbridge Gerry of Massachusetts, "With me it will all be over in a minute. But you, you'll be dancing on air an hour after I'm gone."

William Ellery of Rhode Island contributed greatly to history. He stationed himself in a position where he could watch the face and hands of each signer as he came to the table. He reported that some signed quickly while others stretched out the historic moment dramatically. But in no instance could he identify a single expression of fear. His colleague from Rhode Island, Stephen Hopkins, was past 60 and his hand shook as he signed the Declaration. But Hopkins was still peppery and he snapped, "My hand trembles, but my heart does not!"

These men were human and fallible, and perfection was neither their claim nor their attainment. They were products of the peculiar prejudices of the people of their times. They were very familiar with sectionalism, double-dealing in politics, community fears and nepotism in high office. These 56 men, each in a particular way, represented a genius of colonial American people who had already brought forth something quite new upon this continent.

Even before the Declaration was signed the British had issued a blanket condemnation of all members of Congress, accusing them of treason. They all became objects of a vicious and constant manhunt. The British caught some; others, such as Jefferson, had narrow escapes, and others risked their lives repeatedly in skirmishes and battles. Every man whose family and property came within control of British forces suffered.

For example, the four delegates from New York were men of substantial property, and that fleet of British ships was only miles from their homes when they signed. By that date, the government of New York had already evacuated New York City and moved to White Plains. The four delegates knew their signatures were tantamount to giving away everything they owned.

The British landed three divisions on Long Island August 27. In a bloody battle, Washington's untrained militia was driven back to Harlem Heights. British and Hessian soldiers plundered the mansion of Francis Lewis at Whitestone, set it afire and abducted his wife.

The British overran the extensive properties of William Floyd. His wife and children had fled to Connecticut, where they lived as refugees for seven years without any income. When they returned home, they found their estate "despoiled of almost everything but the naked soil."

Philip Livingston, another signer, came from a baronial New York family and had added to his family wealth a very lucrative import business. All his property in New York City was seized by the British when Washington retreated south to Jersey, and Livingston's town house on Duke Street and his country estate in Brooklyn Heights were also confiscated. His family was driven out and they became refugees. He died in 1778, still working in Congress for the cause, having sold everything that had not been stolen from him, in support of the Revolution.

Lewis Morris of Westchester County, New York, hid and watched while British troops destroyed the timber and crops on his farm and took away all the livestock. He was a Brigadier General in the New York militia during the Revolution.

John Hart of Trenton had been hiding from the British, but took a chance on being captured and went to the bedside of his dying wife. A traitor among the colonists betrayed Hart, and Hessian troops rode into the woods hunting him. They destroyed his gristmill, wrecked his house, and all but pulled it down around Mrs. Hart, who was still on her deathbed.

John Hart evaded his would-be captors and hid in the woods for months. When he was finally able to sneak back home, he found that his wife had died and his 13 children scattered. He died in 1779 without ever seeing any of his family again.

Abraham Clark, a self-made man, gave up two sons as officers in the Revolutionary Army. They were captured and sent to the British prison hulk in New York Harbor. This was the cruel ship *Jersey* where thousands of American captives died.

Dr. John Witherspoon, a Declaration signer, was president of the College of New Jersey at Princeton (later named Princeton University). British troops seized the college and used it as billeting headquarters and staging grounds. They burned Whiterspoon's great college library, much of which he had brought with him from Scotland.

Richard Stockton, a State Supreme Court Justice, had signed and rushed back to his estate near Princeton in an effort to save his wife and children. He and his family found refuge with friends, but a Tory sympathizer betrayed them. Judge Stockton was pulled from bed one night and beaten. He was thrown in jail where he was starved.

He barely survived, but when he went back home, he found the estate had been looted, his furniture and all his possessions burned, his library destroyed and his horses stolen. Richard Stockton died soon after that, and his surviving family had to live off charity.

Of the 56 men who signed the Declaration of Independence, nine died of wounds or hardships during the war. Five were captured, imprisoned and brutally treated. Several lost wives, children or entire family. One lost his 13 children. All were victims of manhunts and were driven from their homes. Twelve signers had their homes burned and 17 lost everything they owned. Not one defected or violated his pledged word.

Their honor and the nation they did so much to create are still intact, but freedom which began on the 4th of July, 1776, came at a high price.

The men who had the most to lose in material things were the first ones to step forward in defense of honor. This was "The Establishment—1776."

The increasing heat of July 4, 1776, climbed at an alarming rate as the Philadelphians packed the State House to hear the results of Thomas Jefferson's committee work. The vote of July 2 had established the fact of independence and now the committee was explaining to the world how the daring conclusion had been reached. The nation had declared her independence from England.

Declaration of Independence

The Declaration of Independence was adopted July 4, 1776, by delegates to the Continental Congress from the thirteen colonies, announcing their separation from England and making them into the United States. It stands today as the basis of our free government. It was eloquently penned by a 33-year-old Virginian, Thomas Jefferson, between June 11 and 28, 1776. A few minor changes were made by Ben Franklin and John Adams. It was presented to the Continental Congress for debate July 4, 1776, accepted July 8, and finally signed August 2. The document is full of Jefferson's fervent spirit and personality, and its ideals were those to which his life was dedicated . . . "that all men are created equal . . . ."

Independence Hall

Originally built as the Pennsylvania State House, the building now called Independence Hall was started in 1732 and completed about 1757.

INDEPENDENCE HALL

In this building the Continental Congress approved the final draft of the Declaration of Independence. On September 17, 1787, the Federal Convention meeting in this building completed its work on the Constitution. To this country and freedom-loving countries all over the world, Pennsylvania State House became Independence Hall because of the patriotism expressed and documents of freedom enacted and written there.

Throughout 1987, the eyes of the world were on Philadelphia as the 200th anniversary of the U. S. Constitution was commemorated in a year-long salute called "We the People 200." The spotlight was focused on Independence Hall, in the heart of America's most historic square mile, where the Founding Fathers gathered during the summer of 1787 to draft this historic document and lay the foundation of the nation.

After two centuries, the focal point of Philadelphia is still Independence National Historical Park. Here stand two of the nation's most precious monuments to freedom, Independence Hall and the Liberty Bell.

Just a few blocks from Independence Hall is Franklin Court, a collection of intriguing monuments to Philadelphia's most famous citizen, Benjamin Franklin.

Liberty Bell

In the hallway of Philadelphia's old State House, now Independence Hall, hangs the Liberty Bell, which, after years of service to the province of Pennsylvania, rang triumphantly to salute the Declaration of Independence in 1776. One of this nation's most cherished symbols of freedom, the Liberty Bell, was silenced on July 8, 1835, when the now famous crack resulted as it tolled for the funeral of Chief Justice John Marshall. Its mighty voice at rest, the Bell still tells a dramatic story of an oppressed people and their successful fight for liberty.

Today, on rare state occasions, the Liberty Bell is tapped with a rubber mallet, and its muted tone has been recorded for posterity. But its real message is symbolic. As the guides tell tens of thousands of visitors to Independence Hall, "The Liberty Bell reminds each of us not only of our rights and privileges but also of our duties and responsibilities."

The Story Behind the

Constitution

By HART ARMSTRONG

The founders of the American Republic were men who possessed a great faith in God and the Bible. When the representatives of the thirteen colonies met in Philadelphia to frame the Constitution, they engaged in three weeks of fruitless wrangling. When it looked as though the meeting might break up in confusion, Benjamin Franklin arose to say,

> Mr. President, I perceive we are not in a position to pursue this business any further. Our blood is too hot. I therefore move you, sir, that we separate for three days, during which time, with a conciliatory spirit, we talk with both parties. If we ever make a Constitution it must be the work of a compromise.
>
> And while I am on my feet, I move you, sir, and I am astonished that it has not been done before, for when we signed the Declaration of Independence we had a chaplain to read the Bible and to pray daily; and I now move that when we meet again we have a chaplain to meet with us and invoke the blessing of Heaven. For, sir, it has been wisely written, "Except the Lord build the city, they labor in vain who build it," and if it be true that a sparrow cannot fall to the ground without His notice, surely a nation cannot rise without His aid.

George Washington's face beamed with joy as he arose to second the motion.

With their minds energized by prayer, these men, after three days, prepared what Gladstone called, "The greatest document ever struck from the brain of man."

Our Constitution is facing its greatest test today, as men who have no concept of the spiritual foundations of our great nation seek to undermine it and to take from us the basic provisions contained in this great document.

Every loyal American should determine that with every power he possesses he will preserve, protect and defend his country and the Constitution which is the foundation for his freedoms.

The Constitution of the United States

One of the greatest documents ever drawn by man was the Constitution of the United States. It embodies everything that civil existence requires. Each individual, irrespective of race or creed or station, shares in its protective rights and justice. The privilege of free speech, religion of choice, voting, etc., are a few of the gifts handed down to us in the blood and sweat of our courageous forefathers. It is another and more effective step toward building and preserving human rights. Its principles have established the most democratic form of Government on the face of the earth.

THE AMERICAN EAGLE

For more than a year the thirteen colonies were simply on a strike against the British Parliament. The revolution was a walk-out. Then the colonies decided to stay out. They organized themselves into a nation and gave their reasons in the resolution of independency passed on July 2, 1776.

Immediately they needed a great seal for official documents, and on July 4, 1776, after ordering the Declaration of Independence printed, the Congress appointed a committee of three to design a great seal.

The three, "Doctor Franklin, Mr. J. Adams and Mr. Jefferson," consulted the French artist Du Simitiere and turned in a report on August 20. Franklin suggested Moses drowning "Pharaoh" in the Red Sea. Jefferson had him leading the Children of Israel through the wilderness. John Adams wanted the choice of Hercules between Virtue and Sloth.

Congress ordered the report "to lie on the table."

Another effort to get a seal was made the next year. This also failed, and Congress muddled along until 1780 when Francis

Hopkinson proposed a design of thirteen stripes and thirteen stars and certain allegorical elements. A committee approved both the drawing and the bill, but Congress dropped the design in order to evade the bill.

In the general chaos, the seal was forgotten for two years more. Then a committee composed of Charles Thomson, Arthur Lee and Elias Boudinot consulted with Mr. William Barton, who proposed the crested eagle. Thomson changed this to "the American bald eagle," then crossed out the "bald." This emblem, with the motto "E pluribus unum" and various other details, was adopted by Congress on June 20, 1782. The ancient motto was a high and dangerous ideal then.

Benjamin Franklin did not, as is often stated, oppose the choice of the eagle, for he was in France at the time. But he regretted the choice and ridiculed the American eagle as a bird of bad moral character, and said that the turkey would have been a better choice as a true native, a nobler bird and braver.

The personality of the American eagle may indeed be most enhanced by distance. But that can be said of almost everybody and everything. There is something about the eagle that uplifts the human heart.

Like our nation itself, for all its faults, our eagle can attain the highest heights and rest there unafraid and unblinded by the sun. He carries our vision and our ideals into the loftiest blue. So let the eagle scream!

Valley Forge,

the Winter Encampment of Washington's Continental Army (December 19, 1777-June 19, 1778) is one of the most sacred spots in American history. Trevelyan, the British historian, has declared Valley Forge the most famous military camp in the world.

* * *

From the crest of Valley Forge Mountain, it is breathtaking to view the historic monuments, statues, log huts and cannon surrounded by vivid golds, rusts and browns of fall foliage. The dogwood trees are as beautiful in their autumn glory as they are in their pink and white splendor of spring. Valley Forge Park in the rolling hills of Eastern Pennsylvania is probably this nation's most beautiful shrine to liberty. But it wasn't to the 11,000 ragged men under Washington's command in December, 1776.

Following a bitter defeat at the Battle of Germantown, a mob of cold, hungry, tired and discouraged men trudged westward along an icy and snow-drifted road some sixteen miles to Valley Forge to set up their winter encampment.

Valley Forge, a little village on the Schuylkill River, got its name from several iron works that produced arms for the Continental Army. The British had occupied the sight a few months earlier and had stripped the area of food and supplies. The retreating army found only frozen, snow-covered fields and a few homes.

George Washington refused to stay in the home that had been leased for his headquarters until every man under his command had a roof over his head. He drew plans for a twelve-man hut and offered a twelve-dollar prize to the group that built its hut first.

Nine hundred cabins were built by mid-January, all

drafty, badly ventilated with dirt floors and wooden fireplaces lined with clay. Food and warm clothing were scarce and many of the men became ill and died of hunger and disease.

Unable to endure the hardships, some of the men deserted. Martha Washington, who had come to spend the winter near her husband, went from hut to hut with a basket of food on her arm and comforted the soldiers who were ill.

Washington was saddened by the suffering of his men and he begged Congress to send money and supplies. It was spring before supplies could be sent, but in February a more important event occurred. Baron von Steuben, a Prussian military expert, arrived with a letter of introduction from Benjamin Franklin. He was the answer to Washington's prayer. He took 100 of Washington's hand-picked men and drilled and trained them into well-disciplined soldiers. They, in turn, trained the rest of the men and the ragged band that retreated to Valley Forge in December marched out a well-trained army in June.

They were greeted with the news that France recognized the American government and sympathized with their cause. The treaty had been signed in February and the Marquis de Lafayette, a prominent Frenchman, became General Washington's aide. Lafayette was a great asset to the American forces in their eventual victory over General Cornwallis and the British army.

General Washington paid this tribute to these valiant men whose courage has been an inspiration to us all. "No history now extant can furnish an instance of an army's suffering such uncommon hardships as ours has done and bearing them with the same patience and fortitude. To see men without clothes to cover their nakedness, without blankets to lie upon, without shoes (for the want of which their marches might be traced by the blood from their feet) and also as often without provisions as with them, marching through the frost and snow and at Christmas taking up their winter quarters within a day's march of the enemy without a murmur, can scarce be paralleled."

George Washington, Lafayette, John Paul Jones—all fought valiantly, courageously and unceasingly. Even the bitter snows of Valley Forge did not stop them. Pressed on every side, within and without—and only defeat in sight—these brave men kept striving, kept fighting, kept hoping.

But how? Why?

Was it just unfair taxes, exploitation and tyranny that kept them on the battlefield?

*No; it was more, much more. The colonists were fighting for freedom of spirit, mind and soul. They wanted more than freedom from tyranny; they wanted freedom **to build** a nation where men could pursue their individual destinies. They had a vision. And that's what carried them through seemingly insurmountable obstacles.*

America's patriots succeeded in freeing us from that particular tyranny. But the fight continues. Each generation, each individual, must carry it on.

Profile of a Traveler

Early one lazy June evening during the first years of the American Revolution, a tall, well-dressed man entered a small patch of woods near the Hudson River.

Judging from his appearance, you would have said he was a man accustomed to exercising authority, and from his bearing you might have concluded that his profession was of a military nature.

Though his horse was panting as if it had been pushed for a considerable distance, one could not justly accuse the rider of inhumanity, for he frequently bent over to caress the patient steed, and seemed to be quite concerned about the animal.

His haste appeared to be activated by necessity rather than sport— as if he feared he was being pursued. Indeed, he confirmed this suspicion as he forsook the main road for a path through the forest.

He was soon forced to dismount, however, since the fast-falling darkness rendered the surrounding objects all but invisible.

To add to his predicament, the darkness was rudely invaded by a quick flash of lightning, and the peaceful atmosphere was suddenly disturbed by an ominous clap of thunder. Before he could reach the shelter of a near-by friendly oak, the exhausted wanderer was drenched to the skin by the resultant downpour.

Not one to be easily discouraged, the victim began to make himself and his horse as comfortable—or, rather as least miserable—as possible for the night, when he chanced to notice a light through the trees.

Encouraged by the prospect of better lodgings, he made his way over the slippery clay and found himself standing at the door of a sturdy farmhouse. A yapping watchdog eliminated the necessity of knocking.

"Who's there?" demanded a voice from inside.

"A friend who has lost his way, and in search of a place of shelter," came the answer.

"Come in, sir," invited the good-hearted home owner. "And whatever my house will afford, you shall have with welcome."

After conducting the newcomer to a room, where his wife was seated, the farmer led the horse to the barn, and there provided for it abundantly.

Upon returning, he greeted the weary traveler with an invitation to dine—an offer which was readily accepted—and the famished guest attacked the meal with a gusto that undermined his dignity.

After dining, he was informed that this was the regular hour the family held evening devotions, and he readily expressed a desire to worship with his hosts.

Devotions completed, the hospitable farmer lit a pine knot and escorted his guest to his sleeping quarters, wished him a good night, and returned to the adjoining room.

"Susan," he confided to his wife, "I like him better for thinking of the Lord, than for all his kind inquiries after our welfare. I wish our Peter had been home from the army, if only to hear this good man talk."

"I am sure," he continued, "General Washington himself could not say more for his country, nor give a better account of the hardships endured by our brave soldiers."

Through the thin partition they could hear the voice of their guest as he engaged in his private devotions. After thanking the Lord for His bountiful mercies and asking His blessings on the inhabitants of the house, he continued:

> And now, Almighty Father, if it be Thy holy will that we should obtain a name and a place among the nations of the earth, grant that we may be enabled to show our gratitude for Thy goodness by our endeavors to fear and obey Thee.
>
> Bless us with wisdom in our councils, success in battle, and let our victories be tempered with humanity. Endow, also, our enemies with enlightened minds, that they may become sensible of their injustice, and willing to restore liberty and peace.
>
> Grant the petition of Thy servant for the sake of Him Thou hast called Thy beloved Son; nevertheless, not my will, but Thine be done. Amen.

Bright and early the following morning the traveler was up, and declining the kind invitation to breakfast with his hosts, explained that it was necessary for him to cross the river immediately.

He offered to pay his friends for their thoughtfulness, but this money was refused. There was no price tag on Christian hospitality.

"Well, sir," he said, "since you will not let me recompense you for your trouble, it is but just that I should inform you on whom you have conferred so many obligations and also add to them by requesting your assistance to cross the river.

"I had been out yesterday, endeavoring to obtain some information respecting our enemy and, being alone, ventured too far from the camp. On my return I was surprised by a foraging party, and only escaped by my knowledge of the woods and fleetness of my horse. My name is George Washington."

—From *The Defender*

Did George Really Cut Down His Father's Cherry Tree?

There are still the very young—and maybe some of the not-so-young—who would like to know how this story started, and if it is true.

House Democrat Carl Albert turned to the Library of Congress and this is what he found:

"Parson Weems," the indefatigable Mason Locke Weems, appears to have been the first to chronicle the tale in print. Weems, a prolific author of "moral tracts," once preached at Pohick church, in whose parish lay Mount Vernon. He later claimed to have been "rector of the Mount Vernon parish."

The story of George and the cherry tree appeared in the fifth edition of his book, *A History of the Life and Death, Virtues and Exploits of General George Washington, Faithfully Taken From Authentic Documents.*

Weems wrote that it was "related to me, by an aged lady, who was a distant relative. It is too valuable to be lost, and too true to be doubted."

You know the story: 6-year-old George was trying out his new hatchet and chopped into a young cherry tree, a favorite of his father.

"I can't tell a lie, Pa; you know I can't tell a lie," Weems relates the youth crying, "I did cut it with my hatchet."

The father replied:

Run to my arms, you dearest boy .... Glad as I, George, that you killed my tree; for you have paid for it a thousandfold. Such an act of heroism in my son is worth more than a thousand trees, though blossomed with silver, and their fruits of purest gold.

Historians have laughed at this story on the virtue of truth as a myth, but is it? The research of the Library of Congress turned up a curious fact.

In 1899, Richard T. H. Halsey in his book, *Pictures of Early New York on Dark Blue Staffordshire Pottery,* made a discovery: an earthen mug made in Germany between 1770 and 1790, was decorated with a quaint illustration of the cherry tree story. A youth dressed in the costume of the continental period was depicted standing near a felled tree. A large hatchet, the letters "G. W." and the numerals "1776" also appeared.

Does this mean the story had been current long before Weems flourished? Was it spread across the Atlantic in Revolutionary times? And does it add more authenticity to the tale?

John T. Rodgers, of the Library of Congress' research division, can only say: "Who can tell? But why not believe it?"

—AP News Release

Washington Said It:

- Of all the dispositions and habits which lead to a political prosperity, religion and morality are indispensable supports.

- I am certainly near the end, and I look forward to the hour of dissolution with perfect resignation.

- Can it be that Providence has not connected the permanent felicity of a nation with its virtue?

- It is impossible to govern the world without God. He must be worse than an infidel that has not gratitude to acknowledge his obligation.

- We can have but little hope of the blessing of God if we insult Him by our blasphemies.

- Let us rely upon the goodness of the cause and the aid of the Supreme Being, in whose hand victory is, to animate and encourage us to noble actions.

- All would have been lost but for that bountiful Providence which has never failed us in the hour of distress.

- Labor to keep alive in your breast that little spark of celestial fire called Conscience.

- Honor and obey your parents, whatever may be their condition.

● Well has it been said, that if there had been no God, mankind would have been obliged to imagine one.

● The propitious smiles of Heaven can never be expected on a nation that disregards the eternal rules of order and right, which Heaven itself has ordained.

● Religion is as necessary to reason as reason is to religion; the one cannot exist without the other.

● Associate with men of good quality if you esteem your own reputation; for it is better to be alone than in bad company.

● Without integrity the finest talent can never gain the respect of the truly valuable part of mankind.

● The love of my company will be the ruling influence of my conduct. Liberty, when it begins to take root, is a plant of rapid growth.

● Knowledge is, in every country, the surest basis of public happiness.

● I hope I shall always possess firmness and virtue enough to maintain what I consider the most enviable of all titles, the character of an honest man.

*   *   *

"A More Glorious Edifice"

In his matchless eulogy on George Washington in 1832, Daniel Webster closed with the following words:

> Other misfortunes may be borne, or their effects overcome. If disastrous wars should sweep our commerce from the ocean, another generation may renew it; if it exhaust our treasury, future industry may replenish it; if it desolate and lay waste our fields, still, under a new cultivation, they will grow green again, and ripen to future harvests.
>
> It were but a trifle even if the walls of yonder Capitol were to crumble, if its lofty pillars should fall, and its gorgeous decorations be all covered by the dust of the valley. All these may be rebuilt.
>
> But who shall reconstruct the fabric of demolished government?
>
> Who shall rear again the well-proportioned columns of constitutional liberty?
>
> Who shall frame together the skillful architecture which unites national sovereignty with States' Rights, Individual Security, and Public Property?
>
> No, if these columns fall, they will be raised not again. Like the Coliseum and the Parthenon, they will be destined to a mournful and a melancholy immortality. Bitterer tears, however, will flow over them than were ever shed over the monuments of Roman or Grecian art; for they will be the monuments of a more glorious edifice than Greece or Rome ever saw, the edifice of CONSTITUTIONAL AMERICAN LIBERTY.

Washington Monument

The Washington Monument, D. C. is the tallest masonry structure in the world—555 feet, 5 $\frac{1}{8}$ inches high. Located on the mall between the Capitol and the Lincoln Memorial.

Mt. Vernon

It is written that George Washington, known as a warrior and statesman, considered himself first of all a planter. He loved his Mt. Vernon plantation, 15 miles south of the Capital, and it occupied his thoughts even at war. Many of his letters contain references to his crops and building. Washington inherited the house from his father but greatly enlarged and improved it, especially after his marriage to Martha Custis. The mansion, named for English Admiral Edward Vernon, has been fully restored and is as it was in Washington's day, even to being planted with the same crops.

In 1831 the bodies of George and Martha Washington were placed in two plain marble sarcophagi and locked in a new tomb, now ivy covered, on a slope overlooking the Potomac.

MOUNT VERNON

A Nation's Strength

What makes a nation's pillars high,
  And its foundations strong?
What makes it mighty to defy
  The foes that round it throng?

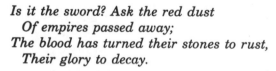

It is not gold. Its kingdoms grand
  Go down in battle shock;
Its shafts are laid on sinking sand,
  Not on abiding rock.

Is it the sword? Ask the red dust
  Of empires passed away;
The blood has turned their stones to rust,
  Their glory to decay.

And is it pride? Ah, that bright crown
  Has seemed to nations sweet;
But God has struck its luster down
  In ashes at His feet.

Not gold but only men can make
  A people great and strong;
Men who for truth and honor's sake
  Stand fast and suffer long.

Brave men who work while others sleep,
  Who dare while others fly—
They build a nation's pillars deep
  And lift them to the sky.

—Ralph Waldo Emerson

"I Pledge Allegiance"

I pledge allegiance
to the flag
of the United States
of America
and to the Republic
for which it stands;
one Nation under God,
indivisible, with liberty
and justice for all.

Betsy Ross and the First U. S. Flag

It was early in the month of June, year 1777, when three men of distinguished bearing visited Betsy Ross at her little upholstering shop at 239 Arch Street in the city of Philadelphia. The tallest and most distinguished of the three was the Commander of the Continental Army, George Washington. The second was Colonel George Ross and the third, Robert Morris, patriot and financier. No doubt it was upon the recommendation of Colonel Ross, uncle to Betsy by her marriage to his nephew, recently deceased, that the pretty widow was chosen to make the first national flag. The selection hardly could have been better for Betsy was skillful with the needle and endowed with a fine taste for color and design.

It may be, as some contend, that the basic idea of the stars and stripes and the colors red, white and blue, was suggested by George Washington. The complete design was quite probably roughed out at the historic visit to the little shop, although Betsy is said to have related that the five-pointed star was her own idea, the original idea being a six-pointed star which Washington thought was easier to make. Betsy seems to have won her preference by folding a piece of paper in a certain manner and after one clip of the scissors unfolded a perfect five-pointed star. This makes for a very interesting and credible story.

With the assistance of two fair friends, and the loan of a navy flag to see how it was hemmed, Betsy was able to deliver the first national flag to Colonel Ross the following day. Our first national flag had thirteen stripes, alternate red and white, and thirteen white stars on a blue field. Mrs. Ross' work met such approval that she received a contract to furnish all the flags for the government. After her death in 1836, the business was carried on for twenty years by her daughter.

There was no change in the number of stars or stripes from the adoption of the original design until 1794, when Congress, in recognition of the admission of Vermont and Kentucky, voted to add two stripes and two stars, one for each of the new states to take effect May 1, 1795. This new flag, with fifteen stripes and fifteen stars, remained unchanged until 1818. More states were being added, and Congress on April 18th of that year voted that the flag should contain thirteen alternate red and white stripes representing the original thirteen states, and that a star for each state should be added on July 4th following its admission. This procedure was followed until forty-eight states were admitted to the Union. The flag remained with forty-eight stars and thirteen stripes until after Alaska, in 1958, and Hawaii in 1959, were admitted to the Union. The current flag has fifty stars and thirteen stripes.

The Betsy Ross House, in which the seamstress fashioned the first Stars and Stripes, still stands at 239 Arch Street, in Philadelphia, around the corner from Old Christ Church where George Washington worshiped. The house is now a national shrine and is visited each year as a point of historic interest.

I am olD GloRy

A Salute to
the Flag

For more than nine score years I have been the banner of hope and freedom for generation after generation of Americans. Born amid the first flames of America's fight for freedom, I am the symbol of a country that has grown from a little group of thirteen colonies to a united nation of fifty sovereign States. Planted firmly on the high pinnacle of American Faith, my gently fluttering folds have proved an inspiration to untold millions. Men have followed me into battle with unwavering courage. They have looked upon me as a symbol of national unity. They have prayed that they and their fellow citizens might continue to enjoy the life, liberty and pursuit of happiness, which have been granted to every American as the heritage of free men. So long as men love liberty more than life itself; so long as they treasure the priceless privileges bought with the blood of our forefathers; so long as the principles of truth, justice and charity for all remain deeply rooted in human hearts, I shall continue to be the enduring banner of the United States of America.

General Rules on Displaying the Flag

The flag should be displayed only from sunrise to sunset on buildings and on stationary flagstaffs in the open. Unless there is some special reason for doing so, the flag should not be flown in rainy or stormy weather. It should be flown especially on legal holidays and other special occasions, but can be flown any day of the year, weather permitting.

On Memorial Day, the flag should fly at half-staff until noon, then be raised to the peak.

It should always be raised briskly and lowered slowly and ceremoniously. In lowering and in raising the flag it must never be allowed to touch the ground.

Prohibited Uses of the Flag

The flag should not be dipped to any person or thing. Should never be displayed with the union down save as a distress signal and never be carried flat or horizontally, but always aloft and free. It should be displayed on a staff—never used as a ceiling covering, receptacle for carrying anything or to cover a statue or monument. It should never be used for advertising purposes—never used as drapery of any sort—never festooned—drawn back, nor up, in folds, but always allowed to fall free.

A 1968 Federal law provides penalties of up to a year's imprisonment or a $1,000 fine, or both, for burning publicly or otherwise desecrating the flag. These were the first Federal penalties, although all the states and the District of Columbia already had laws against flag desecration.

JUST A PIECE
OF CLOTH

In these times of national crises and frustration, we do well to look again to that grand old symbol of so much good and so much liberty and happiness and freedom for us all—the grand old American Flag!

Never was there a period in our history when we stand to gain more by being true to everything it symbolizes and to lose so much by losing faith in all the noble and good things for which it stands.

As Tom Payne once said of the times of the American Revolution, so now, "These are the times that try men's souls."

One of the outstanding men on a Congressional Committee some time ago truthfully said, "One of the greatest responsibilities that can ever rest upon a person is that of passing judgment upon his fellow mortal on his way to the tomb."

This is a time for reserved judgment, for candor and patience, and above all, for deep humility and earnest prayer for our nation and its great needs. Let us not rush to pronounce either guilt or innocence upon its leaders, nor lose faith in its final destiny. God has raised up the American nation to be a missionary bastion to all the world, and we dare not fail that mission. It is a time for re-examination of our own lives and for a deeper look into our own hearts. It is a time for much prayer for our national leaders and for all who bear responsibility.

Here I wish to pass on to you a most beautiful tribute to the American Flag for meditation and thanksgiving as we celebrate this July 4. The author of this excellent tribute is unknown and cannot therefore be credited, but none can doubt that he has left for us an immortal tribute in these words:

That is all it is—just a piece of cloth. But when a little breeze comes along, it stirs and comes to life and flutters and snaps in the wind, all RED, and WHITE, and BLUE! And then you realize that no other piece of cloth could be like it!

It has your whole life wrapped up in it—the meals you eat; the time you spend with your family; the kind of things your boy and girl learn at school; the strange and wonderful thoughts you get in church on Sunday.

Those stars in it—they make you feel just as free as the stars in the wide, deep night. And those stripes—they are bars of blood to any dictator who would try to change this way of life.

Just a piece of cloth, that is all—until you put your soul into it and give it meaning. Then it is a symbol of liberty, and decency, and fair-dealing for everyone. It is just a piece of cloth until we breathe life into it; until we make it stand for everything we believe in, and refuse to live without it.

Again this glad July 4th, ring the bells of liberty, lift aloft the flag of freedom, rejoice in God for all His goodness to this wonderful "land of the free, and the home of the brave."

Let's make America stand for all it was originally intended to stand for. Let us banish our doubts, dismiss our fears, lift high redemption's banner in the name of the Lord, and go into the future with a conqueror's tread, knowing that God will still bless our land with glorious victory if we but trust Him and obey His Word, in confession of sins and weaknesses; in faith for His blessings, and in a holy endeavor to do His good will.

—Dr. William S. Deal

One Nation Under God

In these days when we have seen trials and difficulties at the very highest levels of our government, we need to remember that the United States was founded as and has always been a nation *under God*. Our forefathers realized that without divine guidance their efforts were doomed to failure. So it must always be. With God and in accordance with His purpose, we are a majority; without Him we are nothing.

Perhaps we have become materialistic and selfish, with each person asking, "What's in it for me?"

Let us look at some of the facets of our national life and their relationship to the term *under God*, and see if perhaps we can regain our perspective.

Industry: Without hard work the nation could never have become the power it is. *Under God*, man rested on the seventh day. He worked hard the remainder of the time, putting his trust in Divine Providence, rather than in a desperate drive for just material success. We need to put work into the proper perspective, along with recreation, family living, and community effort.

Economy: Americans of past generations have taught their children, "Waste not, want not," and with this concept *under God* the great majority of Americans have supported themselves and have achieved increasingly higher standards of living. Thrift is a virtue but the size of the nest egg must not become god.

Free enterprise: Economists recognize that our material successes have stemmed from our free enterprise system *under God*, and this must always be, for the same system without God can become exploitation.

Competition: Competition is the essence of our activities *under God*, but simple competition purely for selfish aggrandizement can be vicious and wrong. We are taught by the Son of God the principles of good sportsmanship which we must not ignore even in the keenest competition.

Charity: Charity *under God* is lovingly sharing what we have with the less fortunate. Without it, we have self-righteousness, patronage, pride, encouragement of weakness, and even income tax evasion. God honors charity when it is based upon love and concern for one's fellowman and thanksgiving for our own blessings. In other words, the attitude of the giver determines the worth of the gift, both to donor and recipient.

Liberty: Our forefathers held that liberty is freedom from oppression. To interpret liberty solely as freedom to do as one pleases interferes with the rights of others to the same freedom. This sets up a battle to determine who shall be free rather than the concept that everyone shall be free *under God* so long as one's freedom respects the rights and freedom of others.

Truth: Truth *under God* envisions a return to the basic concept of what truth really is. We have seen the downfall of our President because of a lack of truth. Truth is that eternal verity, not simply what a teacher or a professor proclaims it to be.

This nation, returning to the concept of living and working *under God*, can be the bastion of freedom and democracy for which it was founded.

Lessons are often learned from tragic events; so let it be with Watergate and the actions which followed it.

—Melvin Munn, Commentator

Our National Hymn

Samuel Francis Smith grew up in the north end of Boston, Massachusetts, known as Copps Hill. His life began in 1808, approximately thirty years after the signing of the Declaration of Independence. His home was practically under the eaves of Christ Church (more commonly known as "The Old North Church").

Samuel lived on the very same street where Robert Newman, sexton of "the Old North" in 1775, had lived. Samuel knew that Robert Newman had stealthily climbed the rickety ladder on that fateful night of April 18, 1775, to flash two signals from the belfry tower to indicate to Revere which way the British "redcoats" were planning to advance on Lexington and Concord that night.

Samuel's father's business, making barrels and casks, was at Lewis' Wharf in Boston harbor. Not far from his father's establishment was Griffin's Wharf where the Boston Tea Party had aroused the king's anger sufficiently to close the Port of Boston. Adjacent to Griffin's Wharf was the dock where John Hancock's warehouse had been in 1775. Close by was Constitution Wharf where America's first battleship, "Old Ironsides," was launched in 1791. Samuel knew these stories so well, it almost seemed as if those events had taken place in his lifetime, instead of that of his father.

Inspired, no doubt, by the proximity of these events and places, he wrote the now familiar hymn, "My Country 'Tis of Thee."

Mr. Smith's immortal words continue to inspire millions of Americans. So long as American freedom exists, the song "AMERICA" will be our perpetual heritage.

My country, 'tis of thee,
Sweet land of liberty,
  Of thee I sing;
Land where my fathers died,
Land of the pilgrims' pride,
From every mountain side
  Let freedom ring.

My native country, thee,
Land of the noble free,
  Thy name I love;
I love thy rocks and rills,
Thy woods and templed hills;
My heart with rapture thrills,
Like that above.

Let music swell the breeze,
And ring from all the trees
  Sweet freedom's song;
Let mortal tongues awake;
Let all that breathe partake;
Let rocks their silence break,
  The sound prolong.

Our fathers' God, to Thee,
Author of liberty,
  To Thee we sing,
Long may our Land be bright
With freedom's holy light;
Protect us by Thy might,
  Great God, our King!

America's First Twenty Years

The United States of America grew to greatness in the early years of its existence. Some of the reasons for this meteoric rise in our country's success were our geographical location, our natural resources and our western European cultural heritage.

After giving due credit to these factors, however, we must acknowledge the greatness of our early leaders as the single most important asset which our new republic possessed.

Time after time outstanding leaders came to the fore. From the Declaration of Independence to the Louisiana Purchase, there was always someone to step forward and stand out.

The first great leader of our country was George Washington of Virginia, who gained fame long before there was a United States of America.

After beginning his career as a surveyor at the age of 16, Washington became a military man in 1753 at the age of 21, on the eve of the French and Indian War. Washington performed heroically during this war, being made commander of all Virginia troops with the rank of colonel.

After this war, Washington was alternately a farmer, a member of the House of Burgesses, and a justice of the peace.

In the House of Burgesses, Washington strongly opposed such British measures as the Stamp Tax and the Boston Port Act. In 1775, he was named Commander-in-chief of the Continental Army.

Most people know of Valley Forge and of Washington's gallant leadership throughout the Revolutionary War. Washington also was president of the Constitutional Convention of 1787, and he, of course, became the first President of the United States in 1789.

He served two terms as President and then stepped down, setting a precedent that has prevailed with one exception throughout the years.

Washington's greatest contributions to American life were his devotion to the Constitution and his policy of noninvolvement in the affairs of other countries.

George Washington was indeed the Father of our Country and was "first in war, first in peace, and first in the hearts of his countrymen."

* * *

John Adams, the second President of the United States, was born in Massachusetts in 1735, and his contributions toward freedom were several. In 1765, he fought publicly against the Stamp Act, and in 1766, he wrote newspaper essays for the *Boston Gazette.*

He was a delegate to the first and second Continental Congresses, and he was especially influential in securing the adoption of the Declaration of Independence. He was a minister to Holland and to Great Britain. He served two terms as Vice-President and one as President.

John Adams believed in and fought for independence and freedom at every opportunity.

* * *

Thomas Jefferson, America's great third President, was born in Virginia in 1743. Jefferson showed greatness throughout his life, from the campus to the Presidency.

He was educated at William and Mary College, and in 1767 he was admitted to the Virginia bar, subsequently becoming a successful lawyer. He was elected to the Virginia House of Burgesses in 1769 and for the next six years was a member of every assembly and convention of the colony.

Jefferson was elected to the Continental Congress in 1775 and again in 1776. During the Continental Congress of 1776, he drafted the Declaration of Independence which was adopted by the Congress.

After independence was declared, Jefferson served in the Virginia legislature and as the governor of Virginia. He then served as minister to France. He also used his influence in helping to bring about the Bill of Rights for the Constitution.

In 1789, Jefferson became the first Secretary of State. During his tenure he founded a States' Rights Party. In 1796, he was elected Vice-President of the United States. In 1800, he was elected President.

His greatest achievement as President was the Louisiana Purchase.

Other achievements were the Lewis and Clark Expedition and the naval expeditions against the pirates of Tripoli.

In 1809, he retired to Monticello.

*   *   *

Thus the first twenty years passed. The Revolutionary War had been fought and won; the U. S. Constitution had been written, to which the Bill of Rights had been added; the new government had been established; the Louisiana Purchase had been settled; the western territory was being explored; and the new republic had steered clear of war.

The years 1789 to 1809 were a great twenty years, and these were a great trio of Presidents—Washington, Adams and Jefferson.

—Melvin Munn, Commentator

The Role God Has Played
in the Life of our Nation
and People

Without exception, every President of the United States, at every inauguration, has reminded his constituents of the role God has played in the life of this nation and in the lives of its people.

George Washington, in his first inaugural address, April 30, 1789, said, "We ought to be no less persuaded that the propitious smiles of Heaven can never be expected on a nation that disregards the eternal rules of order and right which Heaven itself has ordained."

In an address before the Senate May 7, 1789, President Washington said, "We commend you, Sir, to the protection of Almighty God." The first proclamation of Thanksgiving found Washington paying unbridled homage and great devotion to God on behalf of his fellow Americans.

Thomas Jefferson, our third President, delivered two inaugural addresses, both on March 4 of 1801 and 1805. In his first inaugural address, Thomas Jefferson said, "And may that Infinite Power which rules the destinies of the universe lead our councils to what is best."

In his second inaugural address he included the statement, "I shall need, too, the favor of that Being in whose hands we are, who led our fathers, as Israel of old, from their native land and planted them in a country flowing with all the necessaries and comforts of life."

President after President, with never a single exception, not only took his oath of office as a servant of God, but enlarged his statement of faith in his inaugural address. Every President has included prayer in official functions and each, in his own way, has sought to follow the dictates of conscience and the Word of God as the worthy leader of faithful men and women.

The preamble to every state constitution expresses gratitude to God and seeks His blessings.

Lincoln's Gettysburg Address, November 19, 1863, hoped, ". . . that this nation, under God, shall have a new birth of freedom."

Freedom Is Not Negotiable

Freedom cannot be put in a bottle, or on a stick like a popsicle, or sliced, or weighed out in pounds. You cannot reduce it to print, or compress it, or define it, or spray it, or explode it. It is teasingly remote in one way, but deeply personal and prescient and immanent in another.

Freedom is a gift of God to all men everywhere, for all time. You can try to sell or exchange it for security, but what you get in the deal is slavery or slow death. The other word is security.

You can try to buy it, but you cannot really buy it, no matter how much security you think you are willing to throw into the scales, for FREEDOM IS NOT NEGOTIABLE!

You have it, that is, whether you like it or not, whether you appreciate it or do not use it. You got it when you were born; you will have it until you die. And no man or state or dictator, no matter how tyrannical, can take it away from you.

The Declaration of Independence states with crystal clarity that all men "are endowed by their Creator with certain unalienable Rights." Here is the precise and exact meaning of the word "unalienable": *freedom cannot be taken away*—ever!

We may not appreciate freedom enough to exercise it. We may not practice it. We may ignore it. We may pass laws or insensibly allow our representatives to pass laws to limit, obscure, or circumvent freedom. But with or without us freedom remains set by the hand of God, fixed in eternity.

We can stand up tall and live up to it, or we can supinely lie down and let it go by without us.

And freedom will surely go by without us if that is the way we want it.

—Donald Haynes in *Freedom News*

Life of
LINCOLN

"I do the very best I know how—the very best I can; and I mean to keep doing so."

Abraham Lincoln's life is the best example of his own words. Consider the chronology of his career:

    1831 - Failed in business
    1832 - Defeated for legislature
    1833 - Again failed in business
    1834 - Elected to legislature
    1835 - Sweetheart died
    1836 - Had nervous breakdown
    1838 - Defeated for speaker
    1840 - Defeated for elector
    1843 - Defeated for Congress
    1846 - Elected to Congress
    1848 - Defeated for Congress
    1855 - Defeated for Senate
    1856 - Defeated for Vice-President
    1858 - Defeated for Senate
    1860 - ELECTED PRESIDENT

Lessons from
LINCOLN
1809-1865

While Abraham Lincoln was cutting wood he often had a book with him and any odd moments were spent in study.

One day when he was sitting on the ground, intently reading a law book, a pompous squire passed by and called out, "Hello, Abe! What doing—studying law? Expect to be President someday?"

"Don't know," replied young Lincoln, "but I am going to get ready for anything God may have for me to do."

◯

Out of a long, painful experience, Abraham Lincoln wrote five sentences which all of us would do well to study:

> If I tried to read, much less answer, all the criticisms made of me and all the attacks leveled against me, this office would have to be closed from all other business. I do the best I know how, the very best I can. And I mean to keep on doing this down to the very end. If the end brings me out all wrong, then the angels swearing would make no difference. If the end brings me out all right, then what is said against me now will not amount to anything.

Mr. Lincoln often preached what he called "a sermon" to his boys. It was: *"Don't drink, don't gamble, don't smoke, don't lie, don't cheat. Love God, love your fellow men, love truth, love virtue, and be happy."*

He taught temperance by example and by precept, and on several occasions suggested to young men not to put their enemy in their mouths to steal away their brains.

While Mr. Lincoln was visiting General Grant's army on the Potomac, an officer asked him to drink a glass of champagne, saying, "Mr. President, this is a certain cure for seasickness." Mr. Lincoln replied that he had seen "many fellows seasick ashore from drinking that vile stuff."

Except for the instructions of his mother, the Bible more powerfully controlled the intellectual development of Lincoln than did all other causes combined. He memorized many of its chapters, and had them perfectly at his command. Early in his professional life he learned that the most useful of all books to the public speaker was the Bible. After 1857 he seldom made a speech which did not contain quotations from the Holy Scriptures.

Abraham Lincoln's love of truth was a distinguishing characteristic, and so great was his reputation as a lawyer that his clients were sure that they would win their cases if they employed him. Yet they knew that if their cases were not fair, it would be useless to consult him.

A lawyer who studied in Mr. Lincoln's office told this story illustrative of his love of justice.

One day, after listening for some time to a client's statement of his case, Mr. Lincoln, who had been staring at the ceiling, suddenly swung around in his chair and said, "Well, you have a pretty good case in technical law, but a pretty bad one in equity and justice. You'll have to get some other fellow to win this case for you. I couldn't do it. All the time, while talking to that jury, I'd be thinking, 'Lincoln, you're a liar,' and I believe I would forget myself and say it out loud."

◯

One day Lincoln was riding in a stage coach, as they rode in those days, in company with a Kentucky colonel. After riding a number of miles together the colonel took a bottle of whiskey out of his pocket and said, "Mr. Lincoln, won't you take a drink with me?"

"No, Colonel, thank you," replied Mr. Lincoln. "I never drink whiskey."

They rode along together for a number of miles more, visiting very pleasantly, when the gentleman from Kentucky reached into his pocket and brought out some cigars, saying: "Now Mr. Lincoln, if you won't take a drink with me, won't you take a smoke with me? Here are some of Kentucky's finest cigars."

"Now, Colonel," said Mr. Lincoln, "you are such a fine, agreeable man to travel with; maybe I ought to take a smoke with you. But before I do so, let me tell you a story, an experience I had when a boy.

"My mother called me to her bed one day when I was about nine. She was sick—very sick—and she said to me, 'Abey, the doctor tells me I am not going to get well. I want you to promise me before I go that you will never use whiskey nor tobacco as long as you live.'

"I promised my mother I never would. Up to this hour, Colonel, I have kept that promise. Now would you advise me to break that promise to my dear mother and take a smoke with you?"

The Colonel put his hand gently on Mr. Lincoln's shoulder and said with a voice trembling with emotion: "No, Mr. Lincoln, I wouldn't have you do it for the world. It was one of the best promises you ever made. I would give a thousand dollars today if I had made my mother a promise like that and had kept it, as you have done."

There is scarcely a man or woman in this country today but what believes that Abraham Lincoln's keeping his promise to his mother helped to make him the great and good and loved man that he was.

◯

Abraham Lincoln left us guidelines to help us in maintaining the framework of democracy in this nation of free men:

   1. You cannot bring about prosperity by discouraging thrift.
   2. You cannot help small men by tearing down big men.
   3. You cannot strengthen the weak by weakening the strong.
   4. You cannot lift the wage earner by pulling down the wage payer.
   5. You cannot help the poor man by destroying the rich.
   6. You cannot keep out of trouble by spending more than your income.
   7. You cannot further brotherhood of man by inciting class hatred.
   8. You cannot establish security on borrowed money.
   9. You cannot build character and courage by taking away man's initiative and independence.
   10. You cannot help men permanently by doing for them what they could and should do for themselves.

Abraham Lincoln
and
footprints
in the snow

One evening two young men, who regularly attended the prayer meeting at the New York Avenue Presbyterian Church, in Washington, D. C., walked into the pastor's study. The room just outside the pastor's study was dark, but they made out the forms of two men, one sitting ahead of the other, near the partly opened door that led to the prayer meeting room. The young men did not give the visitors in the dark a second thought until the following Thursday night when, again on entering the pastor's study, they noticed the same two men in the same positions, the one in front with his head tilted forward listening intently. Their curiosity aroused, the two young men decided to follow the two strangers when the service ended.

When the young men hurried out the door near the pastor's study, fresh footprints in the snow greeted them. One of the young men exclaimed, "One of those men was Abraham Lincoln!" "How do you know?" asked the other. "Look at the size of those footmarks! Lincoln has the largest feet in Washington!" came the answer.

Trotting briskly toward the White House, the two young men arrived just in time to spot the tall, sad-eyed President and a Secret Service man entering the grounds. Immediately the young men raced back to the church where they breathlessly asked the pastor if he knew that President Lincoln had been in the prayer meeting the last two Thursday nights. The pastor begged the young men not to reveal President Lincoln's secret, and it was not until after the assassination that it was told.

The history of the New York Presbyterian Church in Washington, D. C. was recently researched for publication and among the documents found in its archives was a letter signed by President Lincoln. It stated that he had given due consideration to the question of salvation and was now ready to give a public confession of his faith in Jesus Christ and wished to be accepted for membership in the church.

The letter was written on April 13, 1865, and was to be accomplished at the regular services the next Sunday, April 18. On April 14, 1865, Abraham Lincoln was shot by an assassin. Thank God he had trusted Jesus!

Lincoln's Gettysburg Address

Fourscore and seven years ago our fathers brought forth upon this continent a new nation, conceived in liberty, and dedicated to the proposition that all men are created equal. Now we are engaged in a great civil war, testing whether that nation, or any nation so conceived and so dedicated, can long endure. We are met on a great battlefield of that war. We have come to dedicate a portion of that field as a final resting place for those who here gave their lives that that nation might live. It is altogether fitting and proper that we should do this. But in a larger sense we cannot dedicate, we cannot consecrate, we cannot hallow this ground. The brave men, living and dead, who struggled here, have consecrated it far above our power to add or detract. The world will little note, nor long remember, what we say here, but it can never forget what they did here. It is for us, the living, rather to be dedicated here to the unfinished work which they who fought here have thus far so nobly advanced. It is rather for us to be here dedicated to the great task remaining before us, that from these honored dead we take increased devotion to that cause for which they gave the last full measure of devotion; that we here highly resolve that these dead shall not have died in vain; that this nation, under God, shall have a new birth of freedom, and that government of the people, by the people, and for the people, shall not perish from the earth.

*   *   *

Lewis and Clark Expedition (1804-06)

the first U. S. overland expedition to the Pacific coast and back. Conducted by Capt. Meriwether Lewis and Lieut. William Clark. Preparations for the expedition were initiated by President Thomas Jefferson before the Louisiana Purchase

—The Lewis and Clark Expedition.

in 1803. The group started up the Missouri River in three boats on May 14, 1804.

Of the 40 members of the expedition, it is remarkable that only one man died en route, considering they encountered hostile Indians, accidents, sickness, grizzly bears and rattlesnakes, exposure and near starvation. They arrived back at St. Louis in 1806.

Lewis later became governor of the Louisiana Territory, and Clark of the Missouri Territory.

*   *   *

Santa Fe Trail—

famed wagon trail from Independence, Missouri, to Santa Fe, New Mexico, an important commercial route (1821-80). The trail was used by merchant wagon caravans traveling in parallel columns, which, when Indians attacked, could quickly form a circular line of defense.

Transport over the trail was a contributing cause of U. S. seizure of New Mexico in the Mexican War. Use of the trail increased under U. S. rule, especially after the introduction of mail delivery service via stagecoach (1849), but ceased with completion of the Santa Fe Railroad in 1880.

—The Santa Fe Trail.

The Star-Spangled Banner

Composed by Francis Scott Key, September 14, 1814.
Officially adopted as the National Anthem of
the United States, March 3, 1931.

O! say, can you see, by the dawn's early light,
    What so proudly we hail'd at the twilight's last gleaming:
Whose broad stripes and bright stars through the perilous fight,
    O'er the ramparts we watch'd, were so gallantly streaming,
        And the rocket's red glare, the bombs bursting in air,
        Gave proof through the night that our flag was still there;
O, say, does that star-spangled banner yet wave
O'er the land of the free and the home of the brave?

On the shore, dimly seen through the mists of the deep,
    Where the foe's haughty host in dread silence reposes,
What is that which the breeze, o'er the towering steep,
    As it fitfully blows, half conceals, half discloses?
        Now it catches the gleam of the morning's first beam—
        In full glory reflected, now shines in the stream;
'Tis the star-spangled banner—O! long may it wave
O'er the land of the free and the home of the brave!

And where is that band who so vauntingly swore
    That the havoc of war and the battle's confusion
A home and a Country should leave us no more?
    Their blood has wash'd out their foul footstep's pollution.
        No refuge could save the hireling and slave
        From the terror of flight or the gloom of the grave!
And the star-spangled banner in triumph doth wave
O'er the land of the free and the home of the brave.

O! thus be it ever when freemen shall stand
    Between their lov'd homes and the war's desolation!
Blest with vict'ry and peace, may our heav'n rescued land
    Praise the Power that hath made and preserv'd us a nation!
        Then conquer we must, when our cause it is just,
        And this be our motto—"In God is our Trust!"
And the star-spangled banner in triumph shall wave
O'er the land of the free and the home of the brave.

Gold Rush,

rapid influx of fortune-seekers to the site of newly discovered gold deposits. Gold was discovered at Sutter's Mill, California, on January 24, 1848, and the following year about 80,000 forty-niners stampeded to the West Coast. Another gold rush began in 1886 on the Alaskan Yukon; later discoveries were made on the Klondike and at Nome.

—The California Gold Rush.

* * *

James Butler Hickok, "Wild Bill" (1837-1876),

famous lawman who helped bring order to the frontier; his reputation as "the fastest gun in the West" made him a legend in his own time. During the Civil War (1861-1865) he was a Federal scout and Indian fighter. When peace came, he was appointed U. S. marshal out of Ft. Riley, Kansas, with responsibility for maintaining peace over hundreds of square miles of rugged country. In 1876 he was shot from the rear and mortally wounded by Jack McCall, who was convicted and hanged for the deed.

—Wild Bill Hickok.

Alexander Graham Bell (1847-1922),

inventor of the telephone, for which Bell was granted a patent in 1876 and was given the Volta Award by France in 1880.

* * *

—Mr. Bell invents the Telephone.

Daniel Boone (1734-1820),

an American frontiersman and legendary hero who helped blaze a trail through Cumberland Gap, a notch in the Appalachian Mountains near the juncture of Virginia, Tennessee, and Kentucky, in 1775.

A legendary hero even at the time of his death, he became a worldwide figure in 1823 when Lord Byron devoted seven stanzas to him in "Don Juan." Television and motion pictures in the 20th century increased his legendary hero status.

* * *

—Daniel Boone.

Uncle Sam, popular U. S. symbol usually associated with

a cartoon figure having long white hair and chin whiskers and dressed in a swallow-tailed coat, vest, tall hat and striped trousers. His appearance is derived from two earlier symbolic figures in American folklore—Brother Jonathan and Yankee Doodle.

The origin of the term Uncle Sam, though disputed, is usually associated with a businessman from Troy, N. Y., Samuel Wilson, known

©HVAS

affectionately as "Uncle Sam" Wilson. The barrels of beef that he supplied the army during the War of 1812 were stamped "U. S." to indicate government property. This identification is said to have led to the widespread use of the nickname Uncle Sam for the United States; and a resolution passed by Congress in 1961 recognized Wilson as the namesake of the national symbol.

Uncle Sam and his predecessor, Brother Jonathan, were used interchangeably to represent the United States by U. S. cartoonists from the early 1830s to 1861. Cartoonists of the British humor magazine *Punch* helped evolve the modern figure by their drawings of both Brother Jonathan and Uncle Sam as lean, whiskered gentlemen wearing top hats and striped pants.

Probably the first U. S. political cartoonist to crystallize the figure of Uncle Sam was Thomas Nast, beginning in the early 1870s. One of the most familiar treatments in the 20th century was shown in James Montgomery Flagg's World War I recruiting poster, also used in World War II, for which the caption read, "I Want You."

— The Pony Express —

A system of mail delivery by continuous horse and rider relays between St. Joseph, Missouri, and Sacramento, California (April 1860-October 1861).

The Pony Express and its most famous riders, William ("Buffalo Bill") Cody and "Pony Bob" Haslam gave rise to one of the most colorful episodes of the American West. The 1,800-mile route normally required about ten days to cover, with riders changing horses six to eight times between stations, of which there were 157.

The service ceased with the completion of the transcontinental telegraph system.

—Pony Express.

Mine Eyes Have Seen the Glory

PHILIP L. JEWETT

Julia Ward Howe, occupant of room 606 in the Willard Hotel, Washington, D. C., was unable to sleep one night over a hundred years ago in the year 1862.

The Civil War had been raging for almost seven months. The Northern forces had just suffered a stunning defeat at a place called Bull Run. President Lincoln had named General George B. McClellan to head the Union Army.

The Willard Hotel, situated as it was on Pennsylvania Avenue, was the center of activities—the constant parade of troops passing by on the way to the front at all hours of the day and night, singing as they marched. Some of the more fortunate officers were able to stay at the Willard for a few hours of much needed sleep. The hotel was filled, but cots had been set up in the corridors, and these were used by the weary soldiers. Everywhere was the rush and confusion of war. It was in this atmosphere that Julia Ward Howe was inspired to write the famous "The Battle Hymn of the Republic."

What was this small attractive woman doing here in a war-torn city? She was with her husband, Dr. Samuel Gridley Howe, who was in Washington on official business for the Sanitary Commission, now known as the Red Cross.

As Mrs. Howe tossed restlessly about her bed listening to the singing soldiers, the song they sang fascinated her. She liked the cadence, the beat of the music of "John Brown's Body." The lines were repeated three times, then climaxed with the stirring words, "But his soul goes marching on."

Where had the tune originated? Who had written it? Seemingly it was a camp meeting song which had been brought back by some soldiers at Fort Warren, Massachusetts, when they had returned from the South, following the start of the war. It had been written by an unknown Sunday school teacher, William Steffe.

The morning after Mrs. Howe's sleepless night, her husband and his party were invited to watch a review of troops at an army headquarters just south of Washington. While they were there a report came that enemy troops had been sighted. A hasty retreat was ordered.

As Mrs. Howe watched the soldiers march away, compassion rose in her; she noticed how young they were and how brave. Suddenly they broke into the marching song, "John Brown's Body," which she had heard the night before. Dr. Howe's party joined in the singing with Mrs. Howe as the leader. She had had voice training, and her clear, beautiful voice rang out above the others.

"Sing it again, Ma'am," shouted the soldiers.

Later that day she had a sudden inspiration to write some words to fit the music. The few lines that the song contained seemed inadequate. As she sat in her room that night, she heard the tramp of marching feet outside; muffled commands came through the window. Going to the window, she looked out on the long column that was headed for the Potomac—reinforcements for General McClellan. The men were singing.

Mrs. Howe, in addition to being an excellent singer, was also a writer and a poet. An impulse surged upon her; the urge to write overwhelmed her. She crossed the room to a writing desk. Picking up a stub of a pen and some Sanitary Commission stationery, she started to write. Faster and faster she wrote as the words came to her without effort.

They came in measured cadence of marching feet, line by line. Writing swiftly so as not to lose any of her thoughts, Mrs. Howe at last laid down her pen. The song was finished, and it sold a few weeks later for four dollars. It was published in the February 1862 issue of the *Atlantic Monthly*.

That might have ended the story of "The Battle Hymn of the Republic" but for two times when the song was sung with special meaning. It was these two occasions that made the hymn the beloved song that it is.

The first time the song was sung was in the Confederate prison camp at Libby, South Carolina. On this occasion Chaplain Charles McCabe of the 122nd Ohio Volunteers Infantry led the imprisoned soldiers in their singing.

Chaplain McCabe had memorized the song before he had been captured. In the dark days of imprisonment he thought of home and war's end. The guards had told them that the Union forces had suffered a major defeat and that the North was doomed. The prisoners were downhearted, but soon other news came through. The story that the guards had told them was false.

The Union Army had won a decisive victory at an unknown town called Gettysburg. Like a lightning flash the news sped through the prison. Spirits rose to a feverish pitch. Chaplain McCabe rose up and started to sing these words: "Mine eyes have seen the glory. . . ." Soon all the prisoners were singing, and they sang the entire song through to the last thundering chorus: "Glory! Glory! Hallelujah! His truth is marching on."

The other occasion for singing the song was Julia Ward Howe's going to Washington to meet President Lincoln. She was now known as the author of "The Battle Hymn of the Republic." During this meeting she was asked to sing the song that she had written. She had hardly finished the first line when everyone around her had joined with her in the singing. President Lincoln stood with tears in his eyes as the verses that had inspired the Union Army welled throughout the Capitol to unite the people in an intense patriotic feeling.

The song continued to gain popularity in the following years. Although Mrs. Howe wrote other songs and other hymns, none approached the fame and popularity of "The Battle Hymn of the Republic."

—*Lighted Pathway*

The train that brought 5 states into the Union

General U. S. Grant himself rode this "Golden Spike Special" on her historic trip in September, 1883. At Gold Creek, Montana, he drove down the last spike—and Northern Pacific became the first railroad to link the Midwest and the North Pacific Coast.

Soon farmers and fortune-hunters, miners and cattlemen by the trainload were riding the old Lewis and Clark Trail west behind our new iron horse.

Within seven short years, Washington, Idaho, Montana, North and South Dakota joined the Union.

C O U R A G E
Key to Strong Leadership
By DR. LESTER E. PIFER

Standing on the visitors' viewing platform I found myself entranced by the majesty of the huge sculptured faces permanently engraved upon the mountain.

These giants of history—George Washington, Thomas Jefferson, Theodore Roosevelt and Abraham Lincoln—immortalized in granite, keep vigil in the Black Hills of South Dakota, a national memorial visible for sixty miles. Mt. Rushmore does something to me. I am amazed at this, the world's most heroic sculpture, a marvelous display of the skill and talent of the famous Gutzon Borglum. To reflect upon these determined faces and allow the lessons of history and the accomplishments of these men of valor to thrill my soul is a real experience. Each one, a mere man in himself, made his mark in molding this great nation.

George Washington, our first President, is not known primarily for his military genius, though he used his military knowledge to good advantage in the movement of his troops. His stern leadership, discipline and self-

denial gained him deep respect among his men and countrymen. His talent and dedication welded a people into a solid force to bring a new nation into being, bringing life, liberty and freedom to the dwellers of this land. There are many incidents recorded in the early history of our nation of George Washington's faith in God and his dependence upon God as evidenced in his prayer life.

Thomas Jefferson, our third President, whose face appears on Mt. Rushmore as second, was also an outstanding characterization of courage. Jefferson, a statesman, sage, architect of American ideals as well as noble buildings, assumed towering stature when his country needed giants. He wanted to have inscribed on his grave marker (at Monticello), not that he had held great offices, but that he was author of the Declaration of Independence and the Virginia statute for religious freedom, and the father of the University of Virginia. His own words best express his character:

> I have sworn upon the altar of God, eternal hostility against every form of tyranny over the mind of man.

He further stated an important principle:

> Almighty God hath created the mind free. A man has the right to think as he pleases without interference from the government, and that he should possess the comfortable liberty of giving his contributions to the particular pastor whose morals he could make his pattern.

Theodore Roosevelt, our twenty-sixth President, who appears third in Borglum's monument, was a man of strength, tenacity and moral courage. A many-sided man: war hero, writer and a reform politician, he became then the nation's youngest chief executive. He characterized himself as *"a steward of the people, limited only by specific constitutional restrictions."*

A naturalist and great outdoorsman, he possessed a deep faith in a sovereign God, our great Creator.

Abraham Lincoln, our sixteenth President, appears last but more dramatically a characterization of courage than the rest.

Lincoln, son of a Kentucky frontiersman, whose struggle for living and learning earned him the heart of our nation for his wisdom, thrust him into a place of leadership in America's most dire hour. Arising in his early years, taking "freedom" as his stepping stone, he grappled with our nation's greatest complexities.

"Advancement," he insisted, *"is the order of things in a society of equals."*

After driven to frustration by the failure of his generals, Lincoln emerged as a man of prayer, realizing that wisdom comes from God. Like other giants of the past, he had an impetuous courage as revealed in his second inaugural address:

> With malice toward none; with charity for all; with firmness in the right, as God gives us to see the right, let us strive on to finish the work we are in; to bind up the nation's wounds.

In the year 1863 when our youthful nation, less than a hundred years old, faced its greatest crisis, the senate called upon President Lincoln to set aside a national day of "fasting, humiliation and prayer." The President concurred and proclaimed April 30 as a day for personal and national repentance.

> It is the duty of nations as well as of men, to owe their dependence upon the overruling power of God, to confess their sins and trangressions, in humble sorrow, yet with assured hope that geniune repentance will lead to mercy and pardon; and to recognize the sublime truth, announced in the Holy Scriptures and proven by all history, that those nations only are blessed whose God is the Lord.

Lincoln's deep respect for the Almighty God and His sovereign rule over men was expressed to his register of the treasury, L. E. Chittenden:

> That the Almighty does make use of human agencies, and directly intervenes in human affairs, is one of the plainest statements of the Bible. I have had so many evidences of His direction, so many instances when I have been controlled by some other power than my own will, that I cannot doubt that this power comes from above.

As a lad, Lincoln learned to study and memorize the Scriptures. The truth of the Word permeates his speeches, not just as an adornment, but as an integral part of his logic. The biblical phrase, "a house divided against itself cannot stand," became his classic plea for preservation of the Union.

*   *   *

Certainly we need leadership today possessing these outstanding characteristics found in the Mt. Rushmore "giants." As Christians, we ought to insist on such qualities in our politicians. However, it is doubtful whether a nation so apostate and morally bankrupt can produce such.

As I concentrated upon those faces of Mt. Rushmore and reflected upon the leadership they represent, I could see the necessity for these outstanding qualifications in our churches today.

The church is God's agency through which lives can be changed, in which power can be displayed and with which positive spiritual qualities can be produced in practical discipleship and sanctification (Eph. 3:10-12). We need pastoral leadership whose courage and faith is grounded in the Scriptures and whose lives will be permeated with the power of God and the ministry of the Holy Spirit. The fruits of the Spirit (Gal. 5:22-26), exhibited in our leadership, will go far in providing the example we need for living in a crooked and perverse nation (Phil. 2:15, 16).

Moses gave Joshua and the children of Israel excellent advice on this subject.

Victory comes when courage is exhibited to lay hold upon the promises of God (Joshua 1:2-4).

Strong moral and spiritual courage will come when we realize the presence of God in our lives (Joshua 1:5, 6).

The courage to do right and to walk as God desires is to be found in the Word (Joshua 1:7, 8).

Spiritual leadership and courage comes when there is a realization of God's presence in our lives both to do His will and accomplish His purpose (Joshua 1:9).

The Apostle Paul reiterates the same theme: "Therefore, my beloved brethren, be ye steadfast, unmoveable, always abounding in the work of the Lord, forasmuch as ye know that your labour is not in vain in the Lord" (I Cor. 15:58).

* * *

The Story of 10 Poor Boys

● JOHN ADAMS, second President of the United States, was the son of a grocer of very moderate means. The only start he had was a good education.

● ANDREW JACKSON was born in a log hut in North Carolina, and was reared in the pine woods for which the state is famous.

● JAMES K. POLK spent the earlier years of his life helping to dig out a living out of a new farm in North Carolina. He was afterward a clerk in a country store.

● MILLARD FILLMORE was the son of a New York farmer, and his home was a humble one. He learned the business of a clothier.

● JAMES BUCHANAN was born in a small town in the Allegheny Mountains. His father cut the logs and built the house in what was then a wilderness.

● ABRAHAM LINCOLN was the son of a wretchedly poor farmer in Kentucky, and lived in a log cabin until he was twenty-one years old.

● ANDREW JOHNSON was apprenticed to a tailor at the age of ten years by his widowed mother. He was never able to attend school, and picked up all the education he ever had.

● ULYSSES S. GRANT lived the life of a village boy, in a plain house on the banks of the Ohio River, until he was seventeen years of age.

● JAMES A. GARFIELD was born in a log cabin. He worked on the farm until he was strong enough to use carpenter's tools, when he learned the trade. He afterwards worked on a canal.

● GROVER CLEVELAND'S father was a Presbyterian minister with a small salary and a large family. The boys had to earn their living.

Statue of Liberty

Many tears of joy have been shed and will continue to be shed at the sight of the colossal Statue of Liberty in New York Harbor. Homecoming Americans and immigrants alike can hardly refrain from emotion when they realize this statue is welcoming them to the blessings of liberty enjoyed by a country that spreads for thousands of miles before them. It is a welcome to the achievements, to the opportunities and to the greatness of the American way of life which may be seen symbolized impressively in the background of the statue in the famous skyline of New York City.

This famous statue was first proposed soon after the Franco-German War by a group of Frenchmen, who commissioned one of their number, Frederic Auguste Bartholdi, sculptor, to do the work. The U. S. Congress, February 22, 1877, authorized President Hayes to set apart a site on the island, which Bartholdi, on a visit, had suggested. A committee was formed in 1874 to raise funds. In France, 180 cities, forty general councils, many societies and thousands of people contributed $700,000. In the United States, by the aid of "The World," $300,000 was raised for the pedestal.

The head of the statue was completed for the Paris Exposition, in 1878; the forearm had been sent to America and shown at the Centennial Exposition, Philadelphia, in 1876. Thence it was transferred to Madison Square, New York City, where it remained until 1886. On October 24, 1881, the framework and base were put in place in Paris, Levi P. Morton, the American Ambassador, driving the first rivet. The statue was finished in 1883; on July 4, 1884, M. De Lesseps, President of the French Committee, officially presented the statue to Ambassador Morton; on August 5, 1884, the cornerstone of the pedestal was laid; late in June, 1885, the French vessel, Isere, from Rouen, France, landed the statue at New York; the work of putting the parts together was begun in May, 1886; and the statue was unveiled on October 28, 1886.

The statue weighs 450,000 pounds (225 tons); the bronze alone weighs 200,000 pounds, and is 3/16 of an inch thick; 40 persons can stand in the head, and twelve in the torch; number of steps in statue, from pedestal to head, 161; number of rungs in ladder in uplifted right arm, fifty-four.

The pedestal of the statue is eighty-nine feet in height and sixty-two feet square at the base. There are eleven points in the star. Liberty carries in her left arm, pressed against her side, a book representing the Law, which has on it the date, in block letters, July 4, 1776, as meaning Liberty based on Law.

A little theater was installed in the statue in 1935. A large relief map and skyline charts in the upper elevator enable visitors to identify the landmarks and skyscrapers of New York. The statue is visited by more than 250,000 persons in a year.

Nearby Ellis Island, abandoned as an immigration center in 1954 after having served as the gateway to America for 16,000,000, was proclaimed by President Johnson in 1965 part of the Statue of Liberty National Monument.

After several years' renovation, she is now "new" again, proudly welcoming one and all to our shores.

Give me your tired, your poor,
Your huddled masses yearning to breathe free,
The wretched refuse of your teeming shore.
Send these, the homeless, tempest-tost to me—
I lift my lamp beside the golden door!

THE MAN WHO PAID AMERICA'S DEBT OUT OF HIS OWN POCKET!

AFTER THE REVOLUTIONARY WAR, AMERICA OWED FRANCE OVER $2,000,000. SCOTTISH-BORN JAMES SWAN STEPPED FORWARD AND PAID THE ENTIRE DEBT.

Music and singing make for better citizenship. They drive out envy and hate, they unify and inspire. Music is the one common tie between races and nations. —Woodrow Wilson.

Will Rogers said, "America is a great country, but you can't live in it for nothing."

Medal of Honor

After the Revolutionary War, the United States had no decorations until Congress approved the *Medal of Honor* in 1861, during the Civil War. Decorations were unpopular in the United States during the nation's early years because many people considered them symbols of European monarchies. Even the establishment of the Medal of Honor caused much debate. But more than 1,900 U. S. servicemen received it during the Civil War and the Indian Wars. The medal was the only U. S. decoration until World War I. In 1918, Congress restricted the Medal of Honor to persons who perform the most extraordinary acts of heroism. Today, this decoration, often called the *Congressional Medal of Honor,* is the highest U. S. military award.

In God We Trust...

...do we or don't we?

DOES IT MEAN ANYTHING...or doesn't it?

Would another phrase do just as well? Our nation's founders didn't think so!

The men who signed the Constitution... the men—and women—who braved the prairie and the mountain to pioneer our land...they didn't think so.

But what about us? Does this motto on the coin in our pocket guide us...inspire us...strengthen us? Or have we forgotten the power of the faith expressed in these words?

If we are worried about tomorrow, then perhaps the time has come to put aside small things and turn once more to the faith which made our nation great.

Our country's great leaders down through the years have shared a sure belief in God...in themselves...in their fellow men...and in freedom! In crisis and in peace they have placed their faith in God's Wisdom...and in their own ability to work out their problems...and in the great justice of a free people.

Let us do the same today.

PRESIDENTS OF THE UNITED STATES

No.	Name and Politics	Native State	Born	Term	Date of Death
1	George Washington—Federalist	Virginia	1732, Feb. 22	1789-1797	1799, Dec. 14
2	John Adams—Federalist	Massachusetts	1735, Oct. 30	1797-1801	1826, July 4
3	Thomas Jefferson—Dem.-Rep.	Virginia	1743, April 13	1801-1809	1826, July 4
4	James Madison—Dem.-Rep.	Virginia	1751, Mar. 16	1809-1817	1836, June 28
5	James Monroe—Dem.-Rep.	Virginia	1758, April 28	1817-1825	1831, July 4
6	John Quincy Adams—Dem.-Rep.	Massachusetts	1767, July 11	1825-1829	1848, Feb. 23
7	Andrew Jackson—Democrat	S. Carolina	1767, Mar. 15	1829-1837	1845, June 8
8	Martin Van Buren—Democrat	New York	1782, Dec. 5	1837-1841	1862, July 24
9	William Henry Harrison—Whig	Virginia	1773, Feb. 9	1841-1841	1841, April 4
10	John Tyler—Whig	Virginia	1790, Mar. 29	1841-1845	1862, Jan. 18
11	James Knox Polk—Democrat	N. Carolina	1795, Nov. 2	1845-1849	1849, June 15
12	Zachary Taylor—Whig	Virginia	1784, Nov. 24	1849-1850	1850, July 9
13	Millard Fillmore—Whig	New York	1800, Jan. 7	1850-1853	1874, Mar. 8
14	Franklin Pierce—Democrat	New Hampshire	1804, Nov. 23	1853-1857	1869, Oct. 8
15	James Buchanan—Democrat	Pennsylvania	1791, April 23	1857-1861	1868, June 1
16	Abraham Lincoln—Republican	Kentucky	1809, Feb. 12	1861-1865	1865, April 15
17	Andrew Johnson—(see note)	N. Carolina	1808, Dec. 29	1865-1869	1875, July 31
18	Ulysses S. Grant—Republican	Ohio	1822, April 27	1869-1877	1885, July 23
19	Rutherford B. Hayes—Rep.	Ohio	1822, Oct. 4	1877-1881	1893, Jan. 17
20	James Abram Garfield—Rep.	Ohio	1831, Nov. 19	1881-1881	1881, Sept. 19
21	Chester Alan Arthur—Rep.	Vermont	1830, Oct. 5	1881-1885	1886, Nov. 18
22	Grover Cleveland—Democrat	New Jersey	1837, Mar. 18	1885-1889	1908, June 24

23	Benjamin Harrison—Republican	Ohio	1833, Aug.	20	1889-1893	1901, Mar.	13
24	Grover Cleveland—Democrat	New Jersey	1837, Mar.	18	1893-1897	1908, June	24
25	William McKinley—Republican	Ohio	1843, Jan.	29	1897-1901	1901, Sept.	14
26	Theodore Roosevelt—Rep.	New York	1858, Oct.	27	1901-1909	1919, Jan.	6
27	William Howard Taft—Rep.	Ohio	1857, Sept.	15	1909-1913	1930, Mar.	8
28	Woodrow Wilson—Democrat	Virginia	1856, Dec.	28	1913-1921	1924, Feb.	3
29	Warren G. Harding—Rep.	Ohio	1865, Nov.	2	1921-1923	1923, Aug.	2
30	Calvin Coolidge—Republican	Vermont	1872, July	4	1923-1929	1933, Jan.	5
31	Herbert Clark Hoover—Rep.	Iowa	1874, Aug.	10	1929-1933	1964, Oct.	20
32	Franklin D. Roosevelt—Dem.	New York	1882, Jan.	30	1933-1945	1945, April	12
33	Harry S. Truman—Democrat	Missouri	1884, May	8	1945-1953	1972, Dec.	26
34	Dwight D. Eisenhower—Rep.	Texas	1890, Oct.	14	1953-1961	1969, Mar.	28
35	John F. Kennedy—Democrat	Massachusetts	1917, May	29	1961-1963	1963, Nov.	22
36	Lyndon B. Johnson—Democrat	Texas	1908, Aug.	27	1963-1969	1973, Jan.	22
37	Richard M. Nixon—Rep.	California	1913, Jan.	9	1969-1974		
38	Gerald R. Ford—Rep.	Nebraska	1913, July	14	1974-1977		
39	James E. Carter—Dem.	Georgia	1924, Oct.	1	1977-1981		
40	Ronald W. Reagan – Rep	Illinois	1911, Feb.	6	1981-		

According to a ruling of the State Dept., Grover Cleveland is counted twice, as the 22nd and the 24th President, because his two terms were not consecutive. Only 38 individuals have held office.

Andrew Johnson—a Democrat, nominated Vice-President by Republicans and elected with Lincoln.

Cleveland's baptismal name was Stephen Grover; Grant's, Hiram Ulysses; Wilson's, Thomas Woodrow; that of Coolidge, John Calvin. Mr. Truman used the initial S.

Gerald Ford—First President appointed under the 25th Amendment.

AMERICA, WHO IS YOUR KING?

America and independent go together like a horse and carriage. Like bread and butter.

Americans admire a man who goes into business for himself. This is the land of the Horatio Alger heroes. . .the home of an Abraham Lincoln. . .the birthplace of a George Washington Carver.

We love independence.

Every fourth of July we celebrate our independence.

We are proudly independent.

Is such a spirit good?

The answer is: Yes and No.

YES—if it means that we believe in free enterprise. . .the equality of men. . .the right to speak up for what we believe to be true. . .the freedom of the press. . .the right to worship according to the dictate of our hearts, etc., etc.

NO—if it means that we can do as we please. . .if it means that we are NOT our brother's keeper. . .if it means that golds and gadgets can replace God, or science replace the Scriptures.

In summary, independence is wrong if it makes us feel independent of God.

Nations where the woman is dependent on the man—these nations have a very small percentage of divorces. The nations, however, that stress "equal rights" for husbands AND wives have a mounting divorce rate.

And homes where children and teenagers assert their "rights"—you know what centers of discord they are.

Let's face it: man was not meant to be an independent creature. Nor was he made to be a slave. He was created to be happily dependent on God.

All went well until Mr. and Mrs. Adam got too independent, deciding that they didn't need God's law, that they were old enough to do as they pleased. Their fruit, failure and folly stand out as warning signals to any person or nation who thinks it can do as it pleases and live happily ever after.

The eighth chapter of I Samuel is the story of a nation that wanted to declare its independence of God.

"Give us a king over us," Israel shouted at the aged Samuel. "We want to be like all the other nations that have a king to judge them and to go before them in battle."

Heartbroken, godly old Samuel, the senior statesman of that day, told the Lord about the demands of the people. No doubt he was rather surprised at the Lord's reply: "Go ahead, Samuel. Listen to the people. Give them the king they want. Remember, though, Samuel, they are not rejecting you. They are rejecting Me, their God, that I should not reign over them."

No doubt you recall the rest of the story. Israel was given the most handsome, personable man to be their king. His name? King Saul. However, both Israel and Saul paid a bitter price for their independence. And utter disillusionment came upon the people when their own king died a suicide.

I do predict that unless America and the world go back to the humble reliance on God Almighty, our civilization is doomed to be nothing but a moldy crust of bread on the scrapheap of history.

We were not made to be independent of God and His laws. He is the Creator . . . we are only the created ones. Therefore, He has the right to rule over us.

Refuse His rule—and we must accept the wavering wisdom of the Sauls of our day.

Refuse His Christ—and the world will suffer at the hands of the Antichrist.

On this fourth of July, let me lift my voice for the world to hear this question:

Nations of the world—who is your king?

Friend of mine, who is your king?

Make Christ your King—today!

—From *The Log*

A Tribute to the Salvation Army

THE

BONNET

(written in 1981)

1988 marks the 107th anniversary for the Salvation Army's "hand to man and heart to God" endeavors in the United States.

No religious organization has cared for the down-and-outers like these courageous people. Perhaps on the books of Heaven the Salvation Army may have more souls to its credit than most of the other groups. Among some of the great ones you know, or have heard of, are William Colgate, founder of the Colgate Soap Company; John Brown, founder of John Brown's University in Arkansas; John Newton, composer of the song, "Amazing Grace"—to name a few. In appreciation of their noble work which I have seen first hand on most of the globe's land surface, I think it only fitting that we print here a Paul Harvey article entitled, "Bonnet With a Capital B."

* * *

Where would you find two women who would want to wear identical Easter bonnets? In 1880 five women did. Today, more than a million do. No feathers, lace and frippery, this chapeau. It must be austere black—but sturdy enough to protect the wearer from flying brickbats.

For its designer was Catherine Booth. And this Bonnet, essentially unaltered to this day, is regulation apparel for the lady officers of the Salvation Army. The sturdy Bonnet is made of Milan straw and imported silk. Its price, though small compared to high fashion contemporary hats, is nonetheless considerable for a Salvation Army cadet. Yet to the novice, that first Bonnet is worth saving for—for it is symbolic of her "coming of age," spiritually. And for a cadet, Grandmother's Bonnet is the most treasured heirloom imaginable.

In the beginning, the protective Bonnet had a wider, coalscuttle brim. This has been modified. That is, the brim became less wide as the need for protection diminished. The gap in the back of the Bonnet is to allow for the cadet's long hair.

So durable is the traditional Bonnet, and so precious a symbol, that many more than a half century old are still being worn. And however the Bonnet may have been stoned, scorned or ridiculed, it is trusted all over the world.

An anxious mother sending a small son off on his first train trip in Illinois, sighted a Bonnet among the departing passengers. "Would the Bonnet please look after Junior?" It would. The mother, thus reassured and relieved, trustfully waved a goodbye to her son—and the Bonnet.

Foreigners, lost, confused and frightened on a New York street, anxiously eyeing passers-by for a friendly face, suddenly delight to recognize this world symbol of compassion and assistance—the Bonnet. People in trouble anywhere in the world gravitate toward the Bonnet.

The Bonnet has been cursed and crowned with thorns and stained with blood but it has never been disgraced. Indicative of the respect it has earned, this hat has no nickname, either within the Army or without. It is the "Bonnet"—and it's spelled with a capital "B."

It is inevitable in an era of compromise, accommodation and subversion that some would modify the Salvation Army uniform, a few would abandon it. May this Easter Bonnet for any season remain as it is forever!

—Paul Harvey

Not Coming Home

I kin see him now—
    A lad with a boyish grin,
Browned and lightly-bearded,
    With "peach-fuzz" on his chin.
An' his fox-hole conversation
    Belied the weight of war,
As his eyes began to twinkle,
    In spite of din and roar.
"When this here war is over,
    Then I'm a'goin' home,
An' I'm never gonna wander
    Back across this briny foam.
Gonna settle in the rocker—
    Mebbe rock a time er two,
An' when I've rested somewhat,
    I'll find a job tuh do.
An' I'll buy un automobile
    An' I ain't a-goin' ta walk
Any farther than I hafta—
    Mebbe now an' then uh block,
Then mebbe I'll marry Judy
    An' raise a child er two.
We'll build a home together—
    Boy, that's what I'm looking to."
Yup, seems like yesterday
    That lad with boyish grin
Lay all bloody, stilled forever—
    He's not coming home again.
Over there within a valley
    There're crosses, row on row,
An' little flags a flutterin'
    Now thu drums beat sad an' slow.
All the things that boy wanted
    Are yours an' mine today,
An' he gave them up forever—
    Don't ferget that lad today.

                        —R. W. Cooper

Flanders Field...

is a United States military cemetery near Waregem, Belgium. Buried in this cemetery are the bodies of 368 members of the armed forces who died in World War I (1914-1918). Canadian poet John McCrae wrote the famous poem,

In Flanders Fields

In Flanders fields the poppies blow
Between the crosses, row on row,
 That mark our place; and in the sky
 The larks, still bravely singing, fly,
Scarce heard amid the guns below.

We are the Dead. Short days ago
We lived, felt dawn, saw sunset glow,
 Loved and were loved, and now we lie
 In Flanders fields.

Take up our quarrel with the foe:
To you from falling hands we throw
 The torch; be yours to hold it high!
 If ye break faith with us who die
We shall not sleep, though poppies grow
 In Flanders fields.

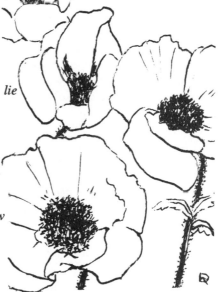

Remembering Our Nation's War Dead

On May 5, 1886, citizens of Waterloo, New York, gathered to honor soldiers who had died in the Civil War. It was the first official *Memorial Day* and had been so proclaimed by Congress. The custom spread. Other citizens in both the North and South sought ways of paying homage to the more than 200,000 wearers of the blue and the gray who had died in that battle.

Since then, the dead of other wars were included, with the result that the veterans of five more wars now are honored on Memorial Day—the Spanish-American War, World Wars I and II, the Korean conflict and the Vietnam War. The American dead of those wars total nearly a half-million.

As we consider all the wars in which Americans have fought, it can be said with certainty that few families in this country have not been touched by at least one of those wars and, in many cases, by several of them.

Nor can we overlook the valiant servicemen and women who have lost their lives in actions during so-called peacetime—the loss of life by 246 Fort Campbell soldiers in the crash in 1986 in Gander, Newfoundland; the 241 Marines who tragically died in Beirut, Lebanon, in 1983 when terrorists bombed their headquarters; the 37 men killed in 1987 aboard the *USS Stark* in the Persian Gulf from the firing of an Iraqi plane, and others.

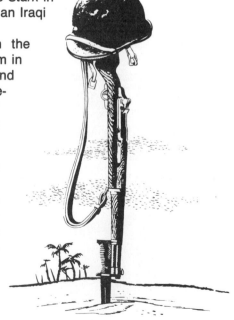

As Americans lay wreaths on the graves of the dead and honor them in other ways, there is a longing and hope that ways can be found to prevent wars in the future. Certainly there can be no doubt but that another major war, if it should come, would quite possibly be the last one, considering the deadly potential of nuclear weapons.

As we pause to remember those who have died protecting our freedom, let us hope that this very fact will serve as a warning to all the people of the world that wars among major nations as we have known them in the past are no longer an option.

—An editorial in *Nashville Banner* on Memorial Day, 1987

THE TOMB OF THE UNKNOWN SOLDIER

One of the most famous monuments in the Arlington National Cemetery outside Washington, D. C., is the TOMB OF THE UNKNOWN SOLDIER. At the tomb a small panel bears the inscription:

"Here rests in honored glory an American Soldier known but to God."

(over)

Nearly three years after the end of World War I, in early 1921, six American soldiers serving in the occupation forces in Germany were ordered to report to a chapel at Chalons-sur-marne. There an American officer met these six men outside the chapel and said, "It is my task to choose one of you to perform a great and sacred duty." He carried a bouquet of roses. He finally chose Sgt. Edward Younger and told him: "In this church are four caskets. In them lie the bodies of four nameless American soldiers. Go into the church. Place a rose on one of the caskets. That is all."

Younger later told the story of walking around the caskets three times. He said: "Suddenly I stopped. It was as though something had pulled me. A voice seemed to say, *This is a pal of yours.* I placed the rose on the coffin in front of me and went back out into the sunlight."

On May 30, 1958, the bodies of two Americans, one of whom died in World War II and one in the Korean War, were returned to the United States and buried next to the Unknown Soldier of World War I.

* * *

Pearl Harbor

On December 7, 1941, Japanese aircraft bombed military installations in Hawaii, touching off the Pacific phase of World War II.

U. S. military fatalities exceeded 2,000. Eight battleships were damaged, three destroyed, and a fourth was capsized. The *USS Arizona* sank, with a loss of 1,102 sailors; this white concrete-steel structure spans the hull of the sunken ship, which was dedicated as a national memorial on May 30, 1962.

Site of *USS Arizona*

★ ★ ★ ★ ★ ★ ★ ★ ★ ★ ★ ★ ★ ★ ★ ★ ★ ★ ★ ★

The Bombing of Hiroshima and Nagasaki

A single B-29 bomber flew over Hiroshima, Japan, on August 6, 1945, at 8:15 in the morning, local time. Hiroshima was chosen because it was a port of embarkation, a convoy assembly site, and the site of an army headquarters, as well as a manufacturing centre. Two-thirds of the city area was destroyed. The combined heat and blast pulverized everything in the explosion's immediate vicinity and killed between 70,000 and 80,000 people besides injuring more than 70,000 others.

The second weapon was dropped on Nagasaki on August 9 killing between 35,000 and 40,000 and injuring a like number. About 50 per cent of that city's area was destroyed.

The next day, August 10, Radio Tokyo broadcast Japan's tentative acceptance of the Potsdam terms of surrender.

A Father's Prayer

By DOUGLAS MACARTHUR

Build me a son, O Lord, who will be strong enough to know when he is weak, and brave enough to face himself when he is afraid; one who will be proud and unbending in honest defeat, humble and gentle in victory.

Build me a son whose wishbone will not be where his backbone should be; a son who will know Thee and that to know himself is the foundation stone of knowledge.

Lead him, I pray, not in the path of ease and comfort, but under the stress and spur of difficulties and challenge. Here let him learn to stand up in the storm; here let him learn compassion for those who fail.

Build me a son whose heart will be clear, whose goal will be high; a son who will master himself before he seeks to master other men; one who will learn to laugh, yet never forget how to weep; one who will reach into the future, yet never forget the past.

And after all these things are his, add, I pray, enough of a sense of humor so that he may always be serious, yet never take himself too seriously. Give him humility, so that he may always remember the simplicity of true greatness, the open mind of true wisdom, the meekness of true strength.

Then I, his father, will dare to whisper, "I have not lived in vain."

December 17, 1903, **Orville Wright,** prone at the controls, made man's first powered flight in a heavier-than-air craft—a 12-second trip above the Kill Devil Hill in North Carolina. Brother Wilbur ran alongside to steady the wing.

—The Wright Brothers

* * *

The Panama Canal

connects Atlantic and Pacific Oceans through the Isthmus of Panama. Ships sailing between the east and west coasts of the United States, which would otherwise be obliged to round Cape Horn, shorten their voyage by 8,000 nautical miles by using the canal.

It was opened to traffic in 1914.

* * *

Charles Augustus Lindbergh, (1902-1974), an

American aviator, made the first solo nonstop flight across the Atlantic Ocean on May 20-21, 1927. Other pilots had crossed the Atlantic before him. But Lindbergh was the first person to do it alone nonstop.

Lindbergh's feat gained him immediate, international fame. The press named him "Lucky Lindy" and the "Lone Eagle." Americans and Europeans idolized the shy, slim young man and showered him with honors.

Lindbergh died of cancer on August 26, 1974, in his home on the Hawaiian island of Maui. He was buried in a churchyard on the eastern edge of the island.

It's Interesting!

—Both Presidents Lincoln and Kennedy were concerned with the issue of Civil Rights.

—Lincoln was elected in 1860; Kennedy in 1960.

—Both were slain on a Friday and in the presence of their wives.

—Both were shot from behind and in the head.

—Their successors, both named Johnson, were Southern Democrats and were both in the Senate.

—Andrew Johnson was born in 1808 and Lyndon Johnson was born in 1908.

—John Wilkes Booth was born in 1839 and Lee Harvey Oswald was born in 1939.

—Booth and Oswald were Southerners favoring unpopular ideas.

—Booth and Oswald were both assassinated before going to trial.

—Both presidents' wives lost children through death while in the White House.

—Lincoln's secretary, Kennedy by name, advised him not to go to the theater.

—Kennedy's secretary, whose name was Lincoln, advised him not to go to Dallas.

—John Wilkes Booth shot Lincoln in a theater and ran to a warehouse; Oswald shot Kennedy from a warehouse and ran to a theater.

—The names Lincoln and Kennedy each contain seven letters.

—The names, Andrew Johnson and Lyndon Johnson, each contain thirteen letters.

—The names, John Wilkes Booth and Lee Harvey Oswald, each contain fifteen letters.

—Does history repeat itself?

—*Sawdust Trail*

Science fiction becomes reality

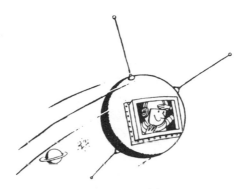

On December 21, 1968, sixty-five years after the Wright Brothers flew the first airplane at Kitty Hawk, three American astronauts, the crew of Apollo 8, journeyed 230,000 miles into space to lunar orbit. Man had taken a voyage previously only written about in science fiction stories. He was entering the far reaches of the universe.

On Christmas Eve, 1968, at 8:48 p.m., CST, astronauts James A. Lovell, William A. Anders and Frank Borman stirred the hearts and minds of all the world as their voices rang out from the depths of outer space.

Borman: *"We are now approaching the lunar sunrise and for all the people back on earth the crew of Apollo 8 has a message that we would like to send to you."*

Anders: *"In the beginning, God created the heaven and the earth. And the earth was without form and void and darkness was upon the face of the deep . . . . "*

Lowell: *"And God called the light day, and the darkness he called night. And the evening and the morning were the first day . . . . "*

Borman: *"And God said, Let the waters under the heavens be gathered together into one place, and the dry land appear: and it was so . . . . "*

All the world listened. In the midst of a sophisticated, scientific and aeronautical achievement, the Bible's message of creation became a memorable part of the mission. The flight plan which had been dreamed of for centuries, had as its most thrilling entry the first verses from God's Word.

On August 6, 1969, atheist Madalyn Murray O'Hair on behalf of herself, her husband, and her "Society of Separationists" filed suit in Austin, Texas, District Court against NASA Administrator Dr. Thomas O. Paine, to prevent

U. S. astronauts on duty from practicing religion "on earth, in space, or around the moon." However, her case was denied by the lower courts and ultimately by the U. S. Supreme Court. Thus, similar readings from God's Word could possibly be a part of future space voyages. "Heaven and earth shall pass away, but my words shall not pass away."

*   *   *

The First Moon Walk

APOLLO 11. July, 1969: this was man's first landing, accomplished by astronauts Neil Armstrong and Edwin Aldrin, on the Sea of Tranquility. They spent 21½ hours on the moon, two hours outside their landing ship "Eagle" bringing home lunar rocks and soil for scientific analysis.

Altogether, twelve astronauts have walked on the moon, in six landings. Eugene A. Cernan and geologist Harrison Schmitt were the last, perhaps in this decade, in the last planned manned flight in the Apollo series.

Our space trips add vast new dimensions to our understanding of the universe. On top of that, the spin-off in technology has brought amazing things to mankind on earth.

* * *

Coincidence?

(In May of 1919 at Dusseldorf, Germany, the Allied Forces obtained a copy of some of the "Communists' Rules for Revolution." Fifty-two years later, the Reds are still following the rules. As you read the following, stop after each item and think about the present-day situation where *you* live—and all around our nation.)

THE RED RULES

A. Corrupt the young; get them away from religion. Get them interested in sex. Make them superficial; destroy their ruggedness.

B. Get control of all means of publicity, thereby;

1. Get people's minds off their government by focusing their attention on athletics, sexy books and plays, and other trivialities.

2. Divide the people into hostile groups by constantly harping on controversial matters of no importance.

3. Destroy the people's faith in their natural leaders by holding the latter up to contempt, ridicule and obloquy.

4. Always preach true democracy, but seize power as fast and ruthlessly as possible.

5. By encouraging government extravagances, destroy its credit, produce fear of inflation with rising prices, and general discontent.

6. Form unnecessary strikes in vital industries, encourage civil disorders, and foster a lenient and soft attitude on the part of government toward such disorders.

7. By specious argument, cause the breakdown of the moral virtues, honesty, sobriety, continence, faith in the pledged word, ruggedness.

8. Cause the registration of all firearms, on some pretext, with a view to confiscating them and leaving the population helpless.

—Selected

When I Was a Boy...

I didn't have a very happy childhood, either...

But nobody worried very much about it. I was too busy, I guess—cutting lawns, shoveling snow, running errands, delivering packages for 10 cents, selling newspapers, doing housecleaning for my mother, and going to school. I passed my grades, too; if I hadn't I'd have had the hide strapped off me.

No one concerned himself about my amusements, either. What fun we had, we made. But if we did any damage like breaking a window in a ball game, we paid for it by working it out.

We never heard these modern phrases like "standard of living," "subsistence level," "minimum requirements." Our standard of living was whatever my father (and after I was about 12, my father and I) earned. I don't suppose people "understand" me and if I had said so, my mother would have asked, "Why should they?" And certainly no one ever gave a thought to my "problems." They were mine, weren't they? Mine to solve. Why should I expect anyone else to bother?

If my father was laid off, we stopped spending on anything but food, and a lot less of that. My dad spent every waking hour looking for work—any work. We lived on savings and when they were gone, we moved in with relatives. If there had been no relatives, when every penny and every salable asset was gone, we would have gone to the only place left—the County Poor House —but that would have been an admission that we couldn't take care of ourselves.

You'll notice in this true story of a typical American family of a few years back, I'm not talking about privileges nor happiness. I guess we didn't have much. But we had something that was infinitely more rewarding—we had self-respect, because whatever we had, however little it was, we earned.

It seems to me that is why America is the strong nation it is today—and it will stay strong only as long as there are enough Americans more interested in earning than getting.

—An American Patriot

Revised Version of *Little Red Riding Hood*

Once upon a time there was a country that was founded by God-fearing men who had principles. This was a land where men had certain rights given to them by their Creator. When man broke the law, he gave up these rights and was punished. We are now living in a land where lawbreakers are rioting in prison because their rights have been violated.

The story of the modern little Red Riding Hood can show what has happened to this wonderful country.

* * *

Once upon a time, in a faraway country, there lived a little girl called little Red Riding Hood. One day her mother asked her to take a basket of fruit to her grandmother who had been ill and lived alone in a cottage in the forest. It happened there was a wolf lurking in the bushes and overheard the conversation. He decided to take a short cut to grandmother's house and get the goodies for himself. The wolf killed the grandmother, then dressed in her night gown and jumped into bed to await the little girl.

When she arrived, he made several nasty suggestions and then tried to grab her. By this time the child was very frightened and ran screaming from the cottage. A woodcutter, working nearby, heard her cries and rushed to the rescue. He killed the wolf with his ax, thereby saving Red Riding Hood's life. All the townspeople hurried to the scene and proclaimed the woodcutter a hero.

But at the inquest several facts emerged:

(1) The wolf had never been advised of his rights.

Cont'd

(2) The woodcutter had made no warning swings before striking the fatal blow.

(3) The Civil Liberties Union stressed the point that, although the act of eating grandma was in bad taste, the wolf was only 'doing his thing' and thus didn't deserve the death penalty.

(4) The SDS contended that the killing of the grandmother should be considered self-defense since she was over 30 and, therefore, couldn't be taken seriously because the wolf was trying to make love, not war.

On the basis of these considerations, it was decided there was no valid basis for charges against the wolf. Moreover, the woodcutter was indicted for unaggravated assault with a deadly weapon: Several nights later, the woodcutter's cottage was burned to the ground.

One year from the date of "the incident at grandma's," her cottage was made a shrine for the wolf who had bled and died there. All the village officials spoke at the dedication but it was Red Riding Hood who gave the most touching tribute. She said that, while she had been selfishly grateful for the woodcutter's intervention, she realized in retrospect that he had over-reacted. As she knelt and placed a wreath in honor of the brave wolf, there wasn't a dry eye in the whole forest.

—Rep. Ed. Eshleman (R-PA)

* * *

What Did He Have to Lose?

A youth was stopped for a traffic violation. The public safety official recognized the odor in the violator's car and it was found that he had a few "joints" with him. He was convicted of a marijuana possession, an automatic felony, and received a suspended sentence. Maybe you think that is a pretty light sentence and something he could take in stride and that he didn't lose much.

Well, all he lost was his right to vote, to own a gun and the right to run for public office.

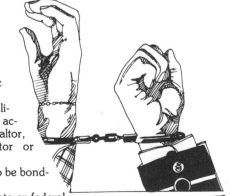

He also lost the chance to ever be a licensed doctor, dentist, certified public accountant, engineer, lawyer, architect, realtor, schoolteacher, barber, funeral director or stockbroker.

He can never get a job where he has to be bonded or licensed.

He can't work for the city, county, state or federal government.

He cannot be admitted to West Point, Annapolis or the Air Force Academy.

That's what he lost.

—Selected